▼ ▼ ▼ ▼ ▼

# The Inner Force

### The Powerhouse
### That Changes Ideas
### Into Action

**Derek Ross**

*as revealed to*

David Barber

▲ ▲ ▲

**The Inner Force**
Derek Ross as revealed to David Barber

**Insight Publishing Ltd**
3a The Maltings
Ross-on-Wye
Herefordshire
HR9 7YB
Phone: 01989-564496
Fax: 01989-565596


Published in association with Cedar Publishing

ISBN: 1-899298-02-9

Cover design by Just Proportion, Louth, Lincolnshire
Printed and bound by Biddles Ltd, Guildford, Surrey

# ◀Contents▶

# Acknowledgements

This book has been a major undertaking in my life. Finding words to express what life has taught me has not been easy. I acknowledge the help and understanding given to me by David Barber, my writer.

A thank you too, to Philip Rudland, who got David and I together many months ago and who prompted this book.

To the many people who have attended my lectures and then encouraged me to 'Put it into book form,' I thank you. I value your support.

I dedicate this book to my grandchildren. Ross is 13 years old and already showing signs of searching for an understanding of what the mind can do. Jemma feels from the inside, a lady in the making. They, and all our children, stand to inherit a world which I, for one, will not be proud to leave them. To them the task, remembering that to put the world right, first get the person right. Many of you will feel, as I do, that we have had our chance to create a better world and have so far been found wanting. But it is not yet too late. It is a sobering thought that, if we all did what we all know must be done, the world would be a better place tomorrow.

Above all, I dedicate this book to my wife Vivienne for whose love, encouragement and understanding I will be eternally grateful.

I love you all,

Derek Ross
Bushey Heath
November 1995

# ◀Foreword▶

This unique book does not contain idle theories; it unfolds the sound, practical, invincible laws of life by which you may open the door to life's supreme prizes. In doing so, you will join those who, under the guidance of Derek Ross, have already soared to superb heights of achievement and discovered how to become joyous and exuberant beings.

Derek Ross is by no means a beginner in the field of Psychology. His formal training came relatively late in life. But he has been a student in the University of Life for over 40 years and therefore he is considered, and rightfully so, to be an established and qualified authority on the subject.

'Passion' is the term I use to describe a quality of excitement that ripens into an intense dedication for his subject. Just a few minutes of listening to one of Derek's seminars will have an electrifying effect on you, and can turn your life around in 24 hours.

The Inner Force is a book that you will come to treasure for years to come.

**Alan Wise**, N.A.C.H.P. Dip H.P.Psych.
*Registered Psychotherapist*
*Harley Street, London*

# ◄Preface►

When Derek Ross first came into my life, he was sharing his experience and knowledge with businesspeople like myself during the course of a two-day seminar. The scene was a town hall, the sombre surroundings of which were hardly conducive to a greatly moving experience.

Yet those two days proved to be two of the most extraordinary of my life. I have been privileged to hear most of the leading speakers on personal motivation, yet here was a man who, without even setting out to be one of them (the seminar was billed as a training course), had grown men crying in the audience—and not only grown men but some of his fellow speakers too, who should by then have become used to him.

Over the next two years, I founded two companies, wrote a best-selling series of instructional books and achieved several long-term ambitions, all the time finding myself inspired by a man to whom I had not even spoken and whom I had not seen since.

Then Fate took a hand. Derek, among many other accomplishments, had previously enjoyed a highly successful career as a professional psychologist in the field of personal motivation, and, having made himself financially independent, he now wanted to give something back to society in the way he knew best: by showing others how to utilise more of their own potential. He would do this by making a series of road-show tours.

However, great speaker though he is, Derek does not claim to be a writer (though I have to say I think he is wrong!). He therefore rejected the idea of a book until, that is, we were brought together at the suggestion of a mutual friend and this project was born.

Derek's message is an important one with exciting implications, not only for individuals seeking to improve their lives through self-development, but for society as a whole.

Parents undertake the most important function in society, which is to prepare the next generation. Yet they receive no real guidance. Every parent must want the best for their children; if parents were taught, using his ideas, how to help their sons and daughters to bring out the best in themselves, the effects on both children and society would be dramatic.

If Derek's techniques were taught in schools then divorce rates, crime, drug abuse and many other social ills would dramatically reduce.

A general application of his teachings throughout society would result in a phenomenal boost to the economy; output, quality of work and profits would show a sharp rise; standards of living in all sectors (particularly amongst the most deprived) would soar; government and bureaucracy would work for the good of the country instead of itself; and we would see justice and common sense in the practice of the law. Why? Because Derek's philosophy is to show people how to take control of their own lives; and people who take control of their own lives also tend to become more critical of social injustice, bad government, bureaucracy and a seriously deficient legal system.

I wanted to write this book for Derek because, after years of studying other programmes, I can confirm that Derek's techniques, ideas and concepts are the most effective I have ever seen. Unlike many teachers on the subject, he has studied the theory in-depth, then taken that knowledge and tempered and moulded it in the light of experience. So take heed of his message because, I promise you, it works. I know.

For this reason, I am immensely proud and privileged to have become involved in Derek's undertaking.

**David Barber**

# ◀Part I▶

# The Quest For Success

# CHAPTER 1

# What Is Self-Development?

> ▼─────────────────────────────
>
> *Throughout recorded history, Man has understood that somewhere there is a source of mighty power which, if he could just find it, would give him the key to the Meaning of Life*
>
> ─────────────────────────────▼

Man has always known that there is a potential somewhere which he can sense without seeing, feel without touching. The Myths and legends of all cultures record personal searches for something of which people are aware but which they cannot fully describe. The only common factor in all these stories is that the power they seek will bestow a special, powerful quality on those who are successful in finding it.

One of these searches in our own culture was for the Holy Grail, the bowl used by Jesus at the Last Supper. According to legend, it was brought to England by Joseph of Arimathea and was lost. Synonymous with the Secret of Life, the Grail became the quest of many knights, including King Arthur.

Later came the alchemists, from whom the word 'chemist' was derived. But their original purpose was not, as you might expect, to invent substances which would improve our daily lot in practical ways; it was either to try to turn base metals into gold, or to discover the elixir of eternal life.

Although many stories and fables (with their modern equivalents in science fiction) tackle the subjects of life without death, the cures for all ills or the sources of wealth or power, the greatest proliferation of these quests is in Greek Mythology with such great stories as Jason and the Golden Fleece, and Ulysses. These exciting myths and legends all involved hardship and danger along the route of their quest and all testify to Man's need to have a purpose in life.

Our heroes were right—there is a power beyond our conscious understanding but they sought it in the wrong place for:

▼———————————————————————

*Our 'Holy Grail' is not on some far distant shore, **but inside each and every one of us***

———————————————————————▼

It is what I call the Inner Force.

## Finding your potential self

What is self-development? It is the journey towards a better self, a more able self, aimed at achieving the success *you* want. And herein lies the first problem: few people know the answer to what they really want. Many people *think* they know, but do they? Let's do a little test to find out. If you will accept the challenge, *before* you read any further why not write down overleaf what you think you want from life and then we will see how accurate you are?

*Please do not read on until you have completed this exercise!*

1. _Love, & security, happiness & understanding in family & marriage, healthy._

2. _Confident, well brought up children happy in & with their lives; being given every good oportunity._

3. _Finacial security for self & family_

4. _To feel that I & my children & spouce have done everything to their best & To help each other_

▼─────────────────────────────

**Success is the quest: self improvement is the journey**

─────────────────────────────▼

Now let's see how you did. Imagine the following situation:

A man was walking past a church one day when he noticed that a funeral was in progress. He was about to walk on when he realised a strange thing: lined all along the road were cars he knew belonged to his close friends and relatives.

'This looks like quite an impressive funeral,' he thought to himself. 'I wonder who it is?' Curiosity got the better of him. He crossed the road and went into

*the church. As it happened, the priest had just con-*
*cluded and his friends and relations were now, one at*
*a time, giving an oration on the deceased. It was then*
*he realised that it was his **own** funeral!*

What would you have people say about you? How
would you like to be remembered? That you had more
money, a big car, a nice house? I doubt it. Whatever
the things are which you would like to have said are
your *real* goals. Some of the other things would be nice
along the way, but they are not the real issue. Remember:

*As you travel life's sweet highway*
*Whatever be your goal,*
*Keep your eyes upon the doughnut*
*And **not** upon the hole!*

Can you think of any greater success in life than to
have your friends and family say what *you **would want***
them to say of you? If you can, let me know! My whole
purpose is to help you to achieve just those things—
those things that you truly want in life. But, for you to
attain your own personal success, we first need to find
out what personal success actually means to you.

So, before you read further, your next exercise is to
complete the question in the box overleaf.

## What can self-development achieve?

Self-development is not about achieving the impossible or the ridiculous. If you want to sit at the sea's
edge, as King Canute did, and command the tide to
stop coming in, you are more likely to drown than to
succeed. Even if you follow my teachings exactly, I

▼ ▼ ▼ ▼ ▼

**If you were able to hear your funeral orations, what four things would you most like your family and friends to say?**

1.


2.


3.


4


*(You can write down more than four if you want)*

Achieving these things is what personal success means to you. Achieving these things is the purpose of our journey together.

Keep this with you at all times and read it often, for living *with* yourself is harder than living *by* yourself.

cannot guarantee that you will be the best parent, become a millionaire, or break the four-minute mile!

▼─────────────────────────────

*All I can guarantee is that, if you apply the concepts of self-development correctly, you will get closer to your goals than you are now*

─────────────────────────────▼

...And the better you apply them, the further you will go and the closer you will get to your goals.

Provided you keep going and working towards your goals, *failure becomes impossible because, by* **keeping** *going, you will always die before you fail.* Most people quit, often at that last hurdle just before they would have received the benefits of their efforts.

▼─────────────────────────────

*If you feel tempted to quit, ask yourself— could this next hurdle also be the last?*

─────────────────────────────▼

### Conviction is the fuel that fires your Inner Force

I said just a moment ago that self-development is not about achieving the impossible but, *if people have enough conviction*, they can and often do achieve the *apparently* impossible. Fakirs have found ways of hammering rods through their bodies without feeling any pain, without shedding any blood and without doing any damage to their tissues or organs.

Who is to say how many people broke the four-minute mile before Roger Bannister because they were being chased by a wild animal?

People have performed superhuman feats of strength or stamina when saving their loved ones—feats which are supposed to be 'impossible'. When I was a young man, I was involved in a car accident. My car finished up on its side, driver's side uppermost. The doors were jammed, but I managed to climb out through the window. I got Karen, my nine month old daughter, out easily enough but my wife was slumped unconscious.

Frantic by now with the fear of the car exploding in flames, I reached down and, one handed, pulled her out in one go. To this day, I do not know from where I found the strength to lift out an inert, nine stone body through a car window. Nor did I suffer from any pulled or painful muscles!

And so the list of 'impossible' feats goes on—you could add your own. Mediocre sportspeople on just one day play as if possessed and do the 'impossible': they outperform a champion, proving that they have the ability but are unable to produce it at will. Suppose they had the ability to do it every day—*to do that they would have to understand and employ this learning system.*

Many of you will want to attract more career success to yourselves. Business life is full of people with apparently no talent or expertise doing the 'impossible' and getting to the top. It happens all the time and sometimes it happens very fast. If you believe by the time that you finished this book, that they got there by luck, or that they happened to be in the right place at the right time, I will guarantee you one thing: YOU will NOT get there. You cultivate your own luck.

# CHAPTER 2

# Lessons
# From Experience

All teachers of self-development have the same problem: the human mind is far more complex than even the most intricate computer. The proof of this is that it is easy to find people who understand how computers work; even if you take the most sophisticated computer yet built, there are many people who could unlock its secrets. But the only Being to fully understand the human mind is the Creator. Mighty intellects from Freud onwards have wrestled with its secrets yet, even today, some of the best brains in the world have fundamental disagreements about the workings of the mind.

If you are deciding whether or not to use a self-development system, it is important to have a look at the author's formal qualifications which allow him the right to speak or write on the subject. After all, would you let someone operate on you if the only surgery they had learnt was from a book? Isn't it just as unwise to let an untrained 'mind surgeon' operate on your mind?

Really successful teachers in the art of personal motivation will need more than theoretical knowledge: they will also need to have proved that their ideas work. I'm afraid that some have only made a name for themselves by telling other people how to succeed—they have never actually been a success themselves in other fields.

A system which has not been tempered in the heat of personal experience can be an empty shell. Therefore, if you can find a teacher with good formal training, good, solid experience of success in other fields and the ability to communicate that information, you have probably chosen an excellent 'mentor'.

*Napoleon Hill spent twenty five years researching his book 'Think and Grow Rich'*, in the process talking to 504 of the greatest achievers of the day. He himself was no mean achiever; he was born in a one-roomed log cabin, yet finished up as an adviser to two Presidents.*

## My credentials as a teacher

I want to show you how success is within the reach of everyone, no matter what their background. I also want you to feel confident that I am qualified to be your teacher and guide. So I would like to share with you my own personal quest for success—how I rose from humble beginnings to realise my dreams in business, in my personal life and in my chosen profession as a psychologist.

So what are my credentials? I had the incredible experience of learning the principles of personal motivation under the direction of Paul J. Meyer, President of Success Motivation Institute Inc. and one of the all-time greats in the field of personal motivation. During the course of our lives, all of us will meet just a few people—perhaps only three or four—who will affect our lives profoundly for either good or bad. Paul was the

---

*Published by the Wilshire Book Company. *If you have not already done so, make this book part of your library!*

one in my life who opened the doors to a fascinating new universe—the limitless power of the human mind. This fired my interest sufficiently for me, at the age of 38, to take a degree in Psychology.

With regard to my business life, I rose from a humble background and virtually no formal education to Managing Director of a number of very successful companies. Twice, starting as a sales assistant, I reached the top in three years. Then followed twice achieving millionaire status through applying the techniques we will talk about, and twice losing that status through not sticking to those techniques! Finally, my wife Vivienne and I started another business which took us from bankruptcy to financial independence in just three years.

When it comes to my personal relationships, two marriages failed because I did not follow the guidelines I have set out here but my third marriage, to Vivienne, has given a whole new meaning to my life. Experience has taught us both how to understand and apply the fundamental concepts of self-development and how to apply them to a relationship.

A relationship like ours resoundingly confounds those critics who say that total commitment to business success cannot coexist with a deeply fulfilling personal relationship. The opposite is in fact true: for the last three years, while we were building up our latest business to create financial independence for ourselves, we had no holidays, worked excessively long hours with no social life and almost always 'cheek by jowl' and yet we were blissfully happy. So, with the right attitude, you can have the best of both worlds—indeed, you can have the best of all the worlds you want and I can point to many other couples who have proved this.

But our marriage transcends other boundaries which are normally seen as 'problems' in personal relationships. Our upbringing could hardly have been more opposite: not only is Vivienne from a strongly Jewish environment and I from an equally emotively strong Roman Catholic tradition, but her background is of public school and wealth (her father was Chairman of several public companies) whereas mine, as you will see, was diametrically different.

Vivienne, of course, was raised in an era when women were expected to stay at home and raise children and her family were no exception. Yet it took her only four years with me to create a reputation as a successful businesswoman and international speaker.

I have also successfully applied the techniques we will discuss in other fields apart from business and personal relationships. I love sport. This led to a successful career as a sports psychologist, advising some of the top twenty international golfers, a world champion snooker player and several Olympic athletes. Professional sports people who are suffering from loss of form are not earning, so you can believe me when I say that they are not going to part with a lot of money to a psychologist unless they can feel the results in themselves!

## The real measure of success

But, although I have experienced my fair measure of success, like all achievers I have had to overcome many difficulties and setbacks. And these have provided some vital lessons which I would like to share.

No matter how well we believe we control our lives, there are outside factors over which we have absolutely no control. No matter who we are, we all have to face failure, disease, death, or the consequences of events entirely beyond our control. This must be accepted as part of normal life.

The point at issue is not that these events occur but *how you react* to them; learning to react positively is the purpose of self-development. Life has to go up and down. You have to go up and down. Your emotions and feelings will go up and down. That is a part of being human—so much so that anyone who is 'down' all the time will end up in a psychiatric hospital. But that is not the end of it; anyone who is 'up' all the time will find themselves in the same place!

There is a danger that self-development counsellors, by concentrating on 'the power of positive thought', might seem to suggest that feeling low or experiencing doubt is something to be ashamed of. The danger of this is that lows or doubts can be stifled or simply not allowed to exist. But using will-power to overcome lows and doubts (rather than learning the proper techniques to overcome them) is dangerous because, far from curing the problem, it can make it worse. Will-power embeds them more deeply in your subconscious mind, from which they can do far more harm because you do not even realise they are there.

The proper course of action is to accept that it is the law of nature for our lives, in common with all living things, to fluctuate between high and low. Indeed, it is unhealthy to the human condition for our emotions not to do so. So we must accept this is natural and understand:

---

▼───────────────────────────

**It is not the circumstances which matter,**
**it is YOUR reaction to them**

───────────────────────────▼

The circumstances are going to happen anyway: you can't stop a war or make the sun come out. It is how you react to them which decides whether they will have an empowering or a debilitating effect on your life. Learning to become personally motivated to positive action is a particularly powerful tool in the area of making sure that one's reaction always remains healthy and positive.

So the greatest test of how healthy our attitude is does not come from personal success, it does not come from business success, it does not come from success in sport, or in our hobbies and pastimes, or in our relationships. It comes from how we react to personal challenges.

### A lesson in overcoming adversity

February 18th, 1993 was a day I shall never forget, for it was on that day that Vivienne and I first faced the trauma which countless couples have faced before and countless more will face in the future. That in no way lessens the shock when your loved one goes in for a routine test and comes out diagnosed as having a malignant cancer.

My relationship with Vivienne is the most important thing in my life—more important than the whole of the rest of my life put together. All of you with a healthy relationship will feel the same about your partner and will recognise the feelings we went through. However strong you are, the shock is devastating and we did what all people do in these situations: we cried together for a while.

But then we realised that, even in the midst of such trauma, we had a choice: did we give into this and allow it to take over our lives, or did we work even more closely together to fully appreciate the wonderful lifestyle we had created for ourselves? Given that we both believed that the proper direction of life is through personal motivation, should we not 'put our belief where our mouth is' and apply the concept to its greatest challenge: how to deal with life-threatening disease?

Vivienne's reaction was incredible. She was about to go to America to achieve one of the milestones of her business life by becoming the first European woman to address a major convention in our industry. So, when the doctor told her she could not go, she told him that her treatment would not start until she got back. If he was that concerned, then he could arrange for an American doctor to treat her while she was over there. But cancel the trip? No way! (What she actually said was less ladylike!)

On her first visit to the after-care clinic, Vivienne realised that being surrounded by people in the waiting room, all discussing and comparing cancers, was the worst possible thing for her attitude. Anyway, going for treatment during the day curtailed her other activities too much. So she demanded, and after much argument got, the first appointment of the day—every day for 172 days!

Her body is now entirely free of cancer. All sign of it has gone. I do not want to take anything away from the wonderful surgeons and hospital staff who looked after her but I am quite sure that her attitude of simply refusing to let it affect her life has been the major factor in her incredibly fast recovery. For instance, she told everyone she met that it was cured—before it was!

There is another important lesson here. We all know that it is at a moment like this, when your choices are thrown into stark relief, that you look back and analyse whether you have used your time wisely. Or have you wasted what could have been precious hours together? Both Vivienne and I analysed our lives in just this way—you can't help it. I am glad to say that, in hindsight, there is very little we would have changed. There is very little we are changing with regard to our future plans.

The only changes we have made are to aim to do some things now rather than in the future. For instance, my plans for the roadshow were intended for later on but I realise now that they mean a great deal to me. And, if they do, why wait? If you are not careful,

▼───────────────────────────────

### *The future has a nasty habit of becoming the past*

───────────────────────────────▼

...And those things you have always wanted to do suddenly become impossible. Hence this book comes out now rather than, 'some day I'll get round to it'.

### A lesson in the power of conviction

As I have said, it is conviction that underlies all success, and I close this chapter with a personal example of conviction in action.

Perhaps the biggest influence on the shape of my life has been my lack of formal education. I say this because I know that many of you will have come from the same origins as I have. The fact that you are reading this book means that you want, as I did, to break free from that environment, and you will be asking the question how.

You may find it helpful if I fill in just a few details of my early life because many of you will relate to this. I hope it will give you the confidence that if I could 'make it', so can you. For those of you who had a better start in life, my message is, if I can 'make it' you definitely can! So I make no apology for these few, brief details of my life.

I was born in Manchester in 1934. Life was not good for my father and, in an effort to find work, he and my mother moved to the South, leaving me with my grandmother.

The bombings of London are well-recorded, those of Manchester less so. Of 140 houses in our street, only four were left standing. Thankfully, one was my grandmother's. It was the Salvation Army which came to our aid, and I can remember the seemingly endless soup queues.

By 1943, my father had saved enough to enable us to be reunited in London. Almost immediately, one of the bombs was pretty good to me—it landed on my school and gave me an eighteen month holiday! People who do not believe in the haphazardness of fate could put that bombing down to the intense visualisations of several hundred boys all willing success on the bomber's aim but, to me, it was several Christmases and birthdays rolled into one.

Missing school at that age severed whatever learning thread I had. Ours was a family which saw schooling as an unnecessary imposition between birth and getting a child out to work and, although I did go back to school for a brief period, I was taken out at age fourteen with little education to show for it. The gratification of missing education is a classic case of 'short term gain, long term pain' and, like many people who have not had the privilege of formal education, I have regretted it ever since.[*]

My father arranged an apprenticeship for me with a local electrician but I was more interested in playing football on the local ash tips.

National Service intervened and opened up for me a large, exciting world which I never knew existed and, from then on, I developed a tremendous thirst for knowledge.

Later, as my experience grew, I found myself becoming more and more attracted to the concept of self-development; more importantly, I found that I had a natural love of it. However, because of my lack of schooling, I had not the confidence to undertake the formal education I felt I should have for a career in that field. I took the problem to my erstwhile mentor, Paul J. Meyer. 'Derek,' Paul asked, 'how much do you want this?' I replied truthfully that I wanted it a hell of a lot!

'Well,' he replied, 'there is one thing for sure. If you don't try for a degree, you definitely won't get one! And, if that is all that is standing in the way of you get-

_____

*In fact, Derek is now one of the best-read people I know.
  (David Barber).

ting what you want "a hell of a lot", why not at least give it a shot?'

But I was still unconvinced. 'Aren't I too old?' I asked.

'How old are you now?'

'Thirty-eight.'

'And the course takes four years?'

'Yes.'

'How old will you be in four years?'

'Forty-two, of course!'

'And, in four years, how old will you be if you don't take the course?'

If you cannot work out whether you want to do something which may take some time, work out how old you will be if you don't do it and work out how old you will be if you do it. If you find a difference, give me a ring!

I am not suggesting that, if you lack as I did, a formal education, you should enrol in a course of higher education. Far from it! I tell you this only to show you that, if you want something, anything, badly enough, there are not many obstacles which you cannot overcome and, by the end of this book, you will know just how you can achieve for yourself anything you want from life.

# CHAPTER 3

# Why People Succeed—
# And Why They Fail

Now that I have shared with you my own personal quest for success, let me summarise the lessons I have learned, and outline the journey we will be taking together.

Throughout my life, the ups have been followed by the downs. That is hardly an earth-shattering revelation because the same is true of everyone; the difference with me was that I simply followed each down with another up because I didn't know any different. I began to wonder why other people didn't do the same, then I realised that they just didn't know how.

This led me to watching other people being successful and to watching myself being successful. I also looked to find out why other people failed and to analyse why my often spectacular successes also turned into crashing failure. And why, when other people failed and then stayed there, did I keep bouncing back so often that my friends started to call me 'Rubber-ball Ross'?

From all of this, two indisputable facts emerged. They applied in every single case I looked at:

▼————————————————————

*1. Success is the result of having a positive Attitude*

————————————————————▼

Many elements make up the right Attitude and we will explore these later. But I would like show you two now:

- Every successful person I have ever looked at has simply refused to be put off or held back

- Most of them acted positively *before* their success materialised.* In other words, they *saw* their success right from the beginning.

▼────────────────────────────────

### 2. Success is the result of right Habits

────────────────────────────────▼

Successful people do not do extraordinary things, they do ordinary things extraordinarily well.

### Why most people never succeed in life

But, as I examined success, I also noticed two important reactions to failure:

- While other people were bemoaning their fate, I was starting again

- While other people looked to outside forces to get them out of trouble, I simply accepted that getting out of trouble was always and entirely going to be the result of my own actions. People often remark that, just when they needed help most, there was no-one there! So I never wasted time waiting for the magical 'they' to intervene.

But why, I asked myself, do other people not do the same? Certain conclusions emerged.

───────────────────

*An example was Vivienne's reaction to her cancer: telling everyone it was cured before it actually was.

*First*, most people look at failure as a result. It is not—it is a journey, just as much as success is. Like success:

▼─────────────────────────────────

*Failure is part of the normal flow of things*

─────────────────────────────────▼

Success and failure are points on Life's compass. Neither is a final destination in itself because life is a journey from one to the other and back again. If you travel north for long enough, one day you will find yourself travelling south.

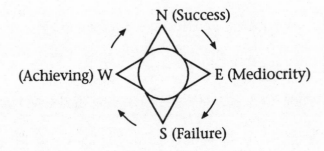

N (Success)

(Achieving) W ◁ ▷ E (Mediocrity)

S (Failure)

*Second*, and this is what causes the first, most people never use their full potential because either they are not aware that they actually have the potential to step out of their problems, or they go down knowing what they should do to stay up—but not doing it!

*Third*, most people believe that talent, skill, intelligence, education, background, being-in-the-right-place-at-the-right-time or a whole host of other things are what make the difference between being average and being successful. In fact:

▼─────────────────────────────────

*The principle difference between being average and being successful is the degree of personal motivation which people bring into play—nothing else—nothing else— NOTHING ELSE!!!*

─────────────────────────────────▼

In other words, the best way to go from being average to being successful is to increase your level of personal motivation. By doing that, you extend your existing potential. Personal development is a science in that, if the ingredients are correct, the outcome is known. An Olympic athlete knows that if he trains his body in certain ways, certain results will follow. We can also learn that, if we develop our minds in certain ways, we will achieve certain results.

This leads to the *fourth* discovery: even if people are aware that the level of personal motivation decides the level of success, they are not aware that it is within the scope of anyone to dramatically increase their level of personal motivation, with equally dramatic results.

*Fifth*, whatever a person is, they can change. People simply do not accept this as a reality. This means that, sadly, the vast majority of people go right through life being the same thing, doing the same thing and getting the same results.

How many times will you hear someone say, 'I can't' or, 'I'm not made like that' or, 'It's OK for him because he's a "natural"'? There is no such thing as a 'natural'.

It is not what Nature or our Creator gives us that counts, *it is how we use it*.

---

> *All skills, all confidence, all desire and all abilities are **developed***

---

You can see from this that the problem is not *'how'*, the problem is *'whether'*. People in the main are simply unaware that they have the option to change. They are unaware that they have the potential to realise their dreams.

So, if you want your dreams to come true, *wake up to the reality of your potential*—or choose to live your life half-asleep.

### Three steps to self-knowledge

There are in fact three stages of achieving knowledge:

---

> *First, people are unaware that they are unaware*

> *Then they become aware that they are unaware*

> *Then they become aware that they are aware*

---

You may now be in the stage of being aware that you are unaware and the whole purpose of this book is to make you aware that you are aware. Once you know that, the golden path to whatever you define as success in the different parts of your life will open up before you.

You, however, will still have to walk that path. It may not be easy. The way may sometimes be hazardous so, to achieve your quest, you will need courage and tenacity. But you must make a start, you must take action! And, to discover the importance of action, please turn to the next chapter...

# CHAPTER 4

# Success Is Activity Waiting To Happen!

Unlike the quests of old, finding your Inner Force is not a hard and dangerous exercise but *something which is within the ability of each and everyone of us to release,* because success is not the science of learning anything new:

▼──────────────────────────

### *Success is developing the things you already have*

──────────────────────────▼

...And isn't it easier to bring out something you already have, rather than have to learn something new?

Many people are frightened by the idea of self-development. Some see it as a mountain to be climbed, as a hard and demanding way of life. But getting the mind fit does not involve the same hard disciplines as moulding yourself into the peak of physical fitness: there is no need for long training runs or punishing sessions in the gym. You see, becoming physically fit always involves pushing the body to limits it has not yet reached. But a child has a positive mental attitude: determination, desire and the will to act. Only after meeting the stumbling blocks of life do these become inhibited or lost. So getting the mind fit is taking it back into a state in which it once was. Doesn't that sound easier?

## Lift yourself above the crowd

Contrary to popular belief, and even (as I write this) in these days of recession, *there are greater opportunities than ever before for people who know how to seek out success.*

Colleges and universities are turning out ever-increasing numbers of graduates but the demand for the *right* people has never been greater; it seems as if there are not enough of the right people to go around.

Never before in history has there been more opportunity than there is now. Companies are competing ruthlessly for the right people. Did you know that good head-hunters charge the equivalent of the whole of the first year's salary, including bonuses and commissions, as a fee? That may sound absurd but companies would not be prepared to pay such sums unless they were desperate for the right people.

The pressure for jobs is not at the top, as you might expect, it is at all levels below the top and it is most crowded at the bottom. Any recruitment consultant will tell you that there are five times as many applicants for, say, a £10,000 a year job as for a £30,000 a year job. It is five times more crowded at the bottom!

So who are the 'right' people these companies seek so ardently? They are the personally motivated individuals. This brings us to the vital law I mentioned earlier:

▼ ─────────────────────────────────────────

*The only difference between people at the
top and those at the bottom are their
levels of Personal Motivation*

───────────────────────────────────────── ▼

*A father arranged for his three sons to be employed by
a fur importer. After a while, he noticed that his sons
were earning significantly different incomes; one son
was being paid £100 a week, another was earning
£200 a week, and the third was on £500 a week. So
he went to the fur dealer and asked, 'Why are you
treating my sons so differently?'*

*'Let me show you,' the fur dealer replied. He called in
the first son and said to him, 'A ship carrying a cargo
of furs has arrived at the docks. Go down to the docks
and take an inventory of what is on board.'*

*The first son went out and very soon returned. 'I did
not need to go to the ship,' he reported, 'because I
have a friend on the docks. So I phoned him and
asked him to count the pelts for me.'*

*Then the fur dealer called in the second son and gave
him the same instruction. The second son took longer
over the task. When he came back, he handed to the
fur dealer a list of all the pelts in the cargo.*

*The third son received the same instruction. By this
time it was getting late, nevertheless, he was away
longer than either of the other two sons.*

*When he finally returned to the office, he said to the
fur dealer, 'There were 200 beaver skins in the cargo.
The owner wanted £2 each for them but I had happened to see a dealer on the dockside and knew that*

he would buy them off me at £2.50. So I have completed that deal. There were 400 minks at £1 each so
I have placed an option on them until Saturday, to
give you a chance to look at them yourself. There
were also 500 assorted pelts of inferior quality and I
knew you would not want those.'

When he left the office, the fur dealer turned to the
father. 'Now you can see that I pay one son £100 a
week because he does not do what he is told. I pay the
second son £200 a week because he does **only** what
he is told. But I pay the third son £500 a week
because he does not need to be told; he is personally
motivated for success.'*

Society caters for non-decision makers. Rightly or
wrongly, it cocoons people by making their decisions
for them. This is an environment which inhibits personal motivation. The result is that the greatest need in
companies is not for knowledgeable people, it is not
for trained people, it is not for educated people, it is for
the *right* people. And the right people are the most
personally motivated people.

▼────────────────────────────

*The right people are the doers, not the
thinkers. The doers lead, the thinkers
follow. The doers employ the thinkers*

────────────────────────────▼

A doer is a decision maker; those who follow wait for
someone else to make their decisions for them.

---

*This story was told to me by Paul J. Meyer.

Doers are not necessarily those with the knowledge. They may not have the technical knowledge but they do know how and where to go and find out. Society does the unemployed no favours. A skilled person cannot find a job because there are too many other people with the same skills chasing too few jobs. But what does society say? 'Get retrained'. So, at great public expense, they get retrained. Guess what? They cannot get jobs with their new skill because there are too many other people with the same skill chasing too few jobs! So what does society say? 'Get trained again'. At that rate, we are going to become a society of highly trained people who never actually do anything.

We should, instead, be teaching people how to increase their levels of personal motivation. Not only will opportunities open up before them, but they will probably finish up better off than they were before! This is not to say that a person should not learn a new skill, but their chances of re-employment increase as their level of personal motivation increases. Your level of activity is decided by your level of personal motivation and one thing I have found is that:

▼────────────────────────────────────

*Activity creates Activity; do something,*
*and other things* **will** *happen*

────────────────────────────────────▼

### Do what you love

Once, after giving a college lecture on this very topic, I was approached by a young man of nineteen. He asked me to explain why personal motivation would achieve more than skill. His interest, he said, was in the computer industry and he was currently undergoing training to fit him for that career. When asked why he had chosen computers, he explained that he enjoyed them and that, although he would like to earn a high income, he was only interested in doing so from an occupation he enjoyed. However, he was concerned about whether he could actually land a job in his chosen career.

'Are there other things you could do, and which you might enjoy just as much?' I asked.

'I can't—I'm trained for nothing else,' he replied. In fact, we are all capable of doing many things and his response showed the limitations caused to people's thinking by the current preoccupation of our employers with 'qualifications'. Once this was explained to him, we got talking and, after much discussion, he remembered that he greatly enjoyed washing his father's car. He got pride from the end result.

'There's your answer!' I said. 'Get a bucket and sponge and clean some cars!'

To my surprise (and I daresay that of his parents), he took me at my word by approaching a massive office complex and arranging to clean the cars of the staff while they were at work.

Today, aged 21, he employs 40 young car cleaners, enjoys a high income with many of the luxuries of life and passes his spare time with his favourite hobby—computers!

### Motivation matters most

You must expand your mind to accept opportunity and never try to make the opportunity fit the size of your mind. How often is the person at the top the best qualified person? How often is the head of department the best qualified person? From my experience as a sports psychologist, I can also ask the question, 'How often is the top sportsperson also the most gifted, the most talented, or even the best technician?' In fact, how often do people appear to succeed by doing it the wrong way? As the saying goes, people succeed by doing the right thing, not by doing things right.

Sport and business are not so very different. The same rules apply whether you want to get to the top in sport or in business, or whether you want to make a success of your personal life or help your children to succeed. If I, as a sports psychologist, was given the choice of working with the most talented sportsperson in the field, or the one with the highest level of personal motivation, I would unhesitatingly choose the latter because here would be the potential winner.

Having said that, personal motivation is not enough to be a top sportsperson; a lot of talent is needed as well. Of course, if I ever found someone who had both the talent and a high level of personal motivation, then I knew I had a world beater!*

In sport, just as in business, it is common to see great natural ability never being fulfilled. But people with high levels of personal motivation are quite rare. *Yet anyone can dramatically raise their level of personal*

---

*The definition of a genius is someone with both massive talent and massive reserves of personal motivation. Fortunately for us lesser mortals, these people are rare! A bountiful Nature seems to want to give everyone a chance to attain success and it often seems to balance natural talent with low levels of personal motivation, or lack of natural ability with high levels of personal motivation.

*motivation*—the only reasons they do not is because they either choose not to or they do not know how...

Life becomes so much more rewarding when you lift yourself out of the crowded areas in the middle and bottom of the market and into the less crowded areas at the top.

I will show you how to raise your level of personal motivation; then it is up to you. Simply having the knowledge will change nothing; committing yourself to *taking action* on that knowledge is what creates change. So sit for a moment and decide before we go any further: 'Am I prepared to take the action necessary?' Because, from now on, I am going to ask you to act.

By reading this far you should now be open minded and receptive to some new information but remember—for things to change *you* have to change, for things to happen you have to *make* them happen.

# CHAPTER 5

# How Should You Use This Book?

It is important that you understand the framework within which we are going to work together to increase your levels of personal motivation. When you have completed this book, we will have seen together:

**1.** That every one of us has limitless potential. We will also discover what holds most people back from realising that potential

**2.** How to understand yourself. Until you understand yourself you cannot decide if, or what, or how, you want to change. We will have discovered how habits are formed—the habits which you can change or improve to achieve what you want from your life

**3.** How to change or improve so that success becomes a habit you no longer need to think about

**4.** How to understand, and accept, the overwhelming importance of goals. You will discover in what areas of life you must, if you wish to be a balanced individual, set goals and how you should go about setting them. Don't worry if other goal-setting programmes have not worked for you because you will find the answer in these pages

**5.** Finally, how to define the conditions in which personal motivation thrives.

The first step in creating those conditions is to *start right now*:

▼————————————————————

*Open your mind. Become a believer in yourself!*

————————————————————▼

### What is your reward for all this?

Well, with the emotional maturity and the positive mental attitude which you will learn to develop, your level of personal motivation can, if you wish, take you to achievements others only dream of, achievements which, up till now, you believed were fantasies!

You will find a pride in yourself which you never knew you had. You will find that you are in control of your life, rather than other influences or people controlling you. You will improve your personal relationships, your health and your enjoyment of life. You will help your children to develop confidence and self-belief and to avoid the crippling effects of unnecessary fear, doubt and uncertainty. This then is the reward.

You will achieve what you want to achieve.

### Start writing your own book!

Take your time in reading this book because I also want you to write your own! Get a notebook and record how the experiences of your own life bear out what I will tell you here. Substituting your own experiences for mine will greatly increase the power of this book to help you to make the changes you want to make. Most of us are not very good at learning from other people's experiences but, hopefully, we are good at learning from our own! So that is what I want you to do.

Each time you write down your own experiences in your notebook, make sure that you put a number in the text of this book so that, when you refer to it later, you can cross-refer to your own book.

### Harness the power of repetition

When you have read right through this book, I want you to read it again, turning it into your own book as you go by relating it to your own experiences and writing them down. Then act on it. To keep you on course, divide the book into twelve to fourteen sections and read just one section each day, reading the same section every day for seven days. In other words, take 12 to 14 weeks to complete the exercise.

If this sounds like a long time, work out how long you have put up so far with those aspects of your life which you do not like and ask yourself, 'Is it worth twelve to fourteen weeks to get rid of those?'

▼────────────────────────────────

*Only when you know by heart both this book and your own, will the valuable lessons be internalised*

────────────────────────────────▼

Internalised means it becomes you and you become it. The only way to internalise is by constant repetition. Constant repetition is a vital part of many tasks.

If I were to ask you to hammer a 6" nail through a block of wood with one blow, you would have to be a mighty strong person; but a child with a toffee hammer can do it if they hit it often enough. Internalising means hear it, speak it and then become it—provided you do it often enough.

Did you know that 62 percent of all ideas are accepted only after they have been presented for the *sixth* time? Give an idea to 100 people, and this is what happens to it *without* constant repetition:

▼————————————————————————

*After 24 hours, 25 have forgotten it*
*After 48 hours, 50 have forgotten it*
*After four days, 85 have forgotten it, and*
*After 16 days, 98 have forgotten it!*

————————————————————————▼

This means that, if you do not apply the technique of spaced repetition learning to this book, after sixteen days you will retain only two percent of it.

*Spaced repetition* is used by advertising agencies because they know that, by repeating a message at intervals (which is what spaced repetition is), they can entirely change your conception of their product. For instance, just look at these words and see what they mean to you:

Polo    Mars

Jaguar    Escort

I'm willing to bet that most of these words do not mean to you what the dictionary says they should! To you, does the word 'jaguar' have its proper meaning of an animal, or has it, through spaced repetition, come to mean a car? Is 'Mars' a planet, or a chocolate bar?

The reason I am asking you to learn in this particular way is because your present internalised beliefs are the result of repetition. The only way to replace them is by the same method. Years of indoctrination are not going to be replaced by a single effort.

Another aid to internalising is to record your notes on a cassette and listen to it as many times as you can in that week. If you have a cassette player in your car use it. When did you last make money from listening to the Top Twenty—or when did the News make you feel good? Give them up—play your messages because these will earn you money, will make you feel good!

For even better results, listen to your tape and read your notes at the same time. This is called multi-sensory learning, which means learning through more than one sense at the same time, and will greatly increase the effect.

You should also add to your notes all the time, continuously elaborating and enlarging your book with your experiences.

Whatever you do, resist the temptation to hurry through the bits you know or don't like. You may think you know something but it will not start to work for you until you have internalised it. Even if you don't like something or find it boring, it is still an essential part of raising your level of personal motivation.

Resist also the temptation to read or listen to everything you can find which has to do with self-development. Too many conflicting ideas will only get in the way at this stage and you will do far better to stick to this one system until you have perfected it. Once it is really working for you, then of course you should broaden your knowledge as much as you can from else-where.

Once you have finished your book, you will find it a great tonic. Whenever you have a 'downer', or find yourself 'feeling blue', *read your book!*

Finally, I want to stress again that your success is going to be always and entirely the result of your own actions. I cannot improve your skill for you; you have to take the responsibility for that yourself. But I can show you a way of removing the obstacles which get in the way of acquiring the skills you need to succeed, and how to replace your present haphazard approach to achieving what you want, by *Planned Action*.

How you use this book is an integral part of that. If you ignore what I have advised you to do in this chapter or take short cuts, you are bound to leave yourself where I found you.

## HOW TO USE THIS BOOK

- Read through this book once
- Then read it again, writing your own book as you go
- To internalise what you have learnt, break the book into 12-14 sections, and read the same section every day for a week before moving on to the next
- So, you should take 12-14 weeks to complete this training
- Spaced repetition is the key to successful internalisation
- Record your notes on a cassette. Play this as often as you can or listen to the cassette while reading your notes. This is known as multi-sensory learning
- Add to your notes all the time, making your book as full and as updated you can
- Don't rush through bits; don't skip the bits you don't like.

# ◀Part II▶

# Potential Unlimited

## Develop The Attitudes That Lead To Success

# CHAPTER 6

# The Unlimited Potential Of Your Mind

In this section, you will learn of the limitless potential which lies within you waiting to be unleashed by the awakening of your Inner Force. You will also learn of the many different ways in which this potential can become blocked, and how you can overcome these blockages.

We begin this task by exploring the unlimited potential of the human mind.

All children are born with a thirst for knowledge which shows as enthusiasm, curiosity, the desire to explore, to learn and to live life to the full. They need these characteristics to progress beyond the child-like state. It is a tragedy that, as we get older, many of us lose these marvellous qualities.

Physical make-up comes from DNA and is given by the parents. There are however no genes to carry personality, flair or abilities. These are learned. Mother smiles and the child copies—so now people say she 'has her mother's smile'. Or she watches her father get his way by losing his temper and copies—hence she develops her father's temper.

However, the fact that each one of us does eventually develop individual mental characteristics must mean that we are actually born with the potential to display all of them. As our life progresses, certain of these characteristics become 'selected' by all the influences we are subjected to, to form the person we are.

For the same reason, we are born with no *individual* personality. The fact that we do eventually develop personalities must mean that we are actually born with the potential to take on *any* personality. There is nothing in our genes which decides, from the moment we are born, whether we are going to be nice or nasty, lively or retiring, honest or criminal, introvert or extrovert, hard-working or lazy. In fact, can you imagine what the effect would be if there was just one DNA molecule programming us for success and we were helpless to influence our own destinies? Even fear or courage are learnt; a toddler would think nothing of crawling across a six-inch plank between two skyscrapers but most adults would not dare!

If we relate what we have just learnt to the subject of this book, this means that there is nothing in our genes which makes us successful or unsuccessful, a leader or led, or destined for wealth or poverty. *All of these things develop later.* In simple terms, we tend to either become what someone else makes of us or we react against this and take charge of our own lives.

Given that a child is born with the potential to do anything, the real problem is that it is the parents who choose the road to success or mediocrity for the child. This is not a criticism of parents. Most want to do their best for their children, but they do not know how and there is no-one to show them. If only parents knew how to choose the success path for their children, the vast majority would do so. Unfortunately, there is no schooling in the most important activity available to human beings—training our future generations—and we are all left to get on with it as best we can.

Without this guidance, parents tend to either do what their own parents did or, less commonly, react quite strongly against it in the way they bring up their own children.

In adult life, too, the spouse or partner exercises influence with comments like, 'Why can't you get a nine-to-five job like everyone else?' or, 'We need the security!'

It is also common that spouses who lack self-esteem find themselves uncomfortable with the raised status in life which is the common outcome of success. If so, this will again exert a negative influence.

▼─────────────────────────────

*Whether or not we are average now, we all have within us the seeds of success waiting to break out*

─────────────────────────────▼

When my grandson, Ross, was younger, he was given a kit to make up. By assembling exactly the same components in different ways, he could choose between making a bell, a buzzer or an alarm. Our brains are the same; we all have the same components but what makes us differ from one another is how all the bits are 'wired up'. However, just like his kit, if there is a loose connection, don't expect it to work!

## The Extraordinary Power
## Of The Universe Of The Human Mind

All scientists and philosophers agree that we use very little of our brain's potential. But they cannot agree how much or how little we use and their figures vary widely: anything from two to twenty percent.

Einstein estimated that he never used more than about ten percent of his mental capacity. If he is right, that means the rest of us are lucky if we ever learn to use more than one or two percent of our mental abilities! The greatest scientists in the world still cannot find out how to unlock that other 90 percent, yet they know that it is there.

If there is a limit to our intellectual capacity, no-one has yet found it.

When people die, autopsies reveal literally millions of unused brain cells. So we all have the potential to be, perhaps not geniuses* or world-beaters, but definitely much better than we are!

Is not the task of self-improvement a simple one compared to understanding a power capable of creating and curing illness?

---

### Girl who refused to die is given a new heart at last

A girl had a heart transplant operation early yesterday *seven weeks* after doctors gave her *72 hours* to live. Doctors believed they had only three days to find a new heart. But Wendy Walker, 10, would not give up. Mr. Hilton the surgeon said: 'She is a remarkable fighter. I went on holiday last week and I did not expect her to be here when I got back.'

---

*Although the latest research indicates that, if people are properly taught from an early enough age, it is possible that, by today's standards, they could all be turned into geniuses.

Some people don't give in. Some people take charge of their own lives. Well done Wendy!*

Would you like to learn how to take charge of *your* life? If the idea excites you, your next step is to understand the Law of Abundance...

---

*Extract from a report in *The Daily Express*. All emphases are the author's.

# CHAPTER 7

# The Law Of Abundance

How many of the people you know would you describe as successful? Is it five? Or ten? Or twenty? Whatever you say, they are going to be in the minority.

The one thing you will notice about all of them is that they have high levels of personal motivation. You see, these successful people are already using the power of personal motivation, often without even knowing it exists.

Others may have some idea but they don't know what to call it, or even how to describe it very well. They make comments like, 'I can't help it'. 'I feel as if I am being driven by something outside of me' (actually, it is *inside* them). 'I can't leave a job half done' or, 'I don't know why, but all I know is that I have *got* to do it!'

Although they are getting close, what they are really talking about is the *effect* of personal motivation, which is a powerful sense of purpose, not about personal motivation itself. In other words, a high level of personal motivation *creates* a sense of purpose. By accident, they have found a driving force.

### The starting point for success

As a preparation for my roadshow, I asked some top people if they could tell me why they had succeeded. None of them could.

Well, the first thing they needed to believe before they could start to succeed was that, whatever it was they wanted, there must be enough of it around for themselves to have a share.

The moment people actually see the wonderful things around them and ask, 'Why not me?', they are starting to recognise the Law of Abundance. When they see something on TV they want badly enough, they will raise their level of personal motivation to have it. If they want a particular holiday badly enough, they will become motivated to save up for it, or take a part-time job to pay for it. They will find a way. Once people recognise that something is actually available, their attitude changes and the quest is on.

People steal because they believe that they cannot acquire what they want in any other way. A person who believes in the Law of Abundance has no need to steal. Getting what you want through directing the force of personal motivation is a lot easier than stealing, a lot more effective than stealing, a lot safer—and you get to keep it!

If, as part of their prison sentences, offenders were taught to believe in the Law of Abundance, instead of being belittled and humiliated, the incidence of re-offending would drop dramatically. If your children were taught these principles as part of their school curriculum, if they were taught how to face the future instead of copying the past, the crime rate would show a dramatic drop. Including these ideas as part of their schooling would make a dramatic difference to their success in life—and not just in their careers but in their personal lives as well.

The person who acquires material opulence, spiritual generosity or business status is the person who believes that there is plenty for everyone.

▼────────────────────────────────

*You will attract unto you that which you think most about*

────────────────────────────────▼

## Abundance is everywhere in Nature

The Law of Abundance is a law of Nature. Just look and see it for yourself. Do you marvel at the abundance of flowers and wildlife around us? Even if mankind continues on its destructive path, nature will still offer an abundance of flora and fauna. Look at the heavens, filled with too many stars for us to count and, for each star we can see, there are countless times as many we cannot see!

Even though we pollute them, the rivers and streams of the world are full of life. The oceans are full of marine creatures of every description. Pick up a handful of sand on the beach and it would take you all day to count the grains. Now think of how many handfuls there are on that one beach. Now think of all the beaches in the world.

All the minerals we have ever mined are just a handful compared to what is under the sea, protected because we do not yet have the technology to mine them economically. Even if we were to use up all the minerals on earth, have you any idea of the bountiful quantities available in the universe? Have you any doubt that Man will not one day find an economical way of mining them?

The world is not designed to hold back, it is designed to give. That is the Plan of Creation.

▼――――――――――――――――――――――――――――

*We accept the abundance of the universe all round us but we seem to be unable to accept the abundance within each and every one of us*

――――――――――――――――――――――――――――▼

### Drink at the fountain of life

We are Nature's finest creation. You are a unique and special act of creation. There are four and a half billion people in the world and yet you are instantly recognisable amongst all of them. It is estimated that 40 to 60 billion people have existed since the dawn of time, yet not one has your finger-prints, not one has your DNA make-up.

Man is an infinitesimally tiny fraction of all the living organisms there are on this planet, yet we are the only creatures that are capable of abstract thought, of complex communication, of mathematical calculation. Tiny though we are to the infinite whole, Man is the only creature to have been given the privilege (and privilege it is) of being able to control and order the world around itself, *yet we neglect the abundance within each of us!* Why?

Most people come to the fountain of life with a teaspoon. If you want success, bring a barrel! Most of us ask too little of life, for which we pay a heavy price. Remember:

▼────────────────────────────────────────

### *You get what you expect!!*

────────────────────────────────────────▼

If you fail to use a faculty which a generous Nature has given to you then, just like an unused muscle, it will waste away. Underground, in lakes so deep that no light can penetrate, there are fish with no eyes. They stopped using them, so Nature took their use away.

There are only three primary colours. Do you find painters complaining because they have no choice? There are only eight musical notes, yet there has been more music written in the last twenty years than in the whole of previous history! There are only 26 letters of the alphabet and every single word has been used millions of times, yet you don't find writers complaining that 'there is nothing left to write'!

If painters, composers and writers accepted lack, they would create nothing. They are only able to create because they accept the Law of Abundance. So must we.

Nature has given us the power to create more than any other form of life. But, if you do not accept the Law of Abundance, you will create nothing with the abundant power you have within you. You will always feel that there is none left over for you.

It is well established that success-oriented people seem to attract to themselves what other people call coincidences. But these coincidences are so frequent and so specifically aimed at what the individual needs at that time, that they cannot be explained away so easily. Maybe this is what Voltaire meant when he said,

'Beware on what you set your heart, for you will surely get it.'

The people who suffer most from illness are often those who talk most about it. They seem to go from one physical problem to the next! Equally, those who believe in lack do seem to 'tune in' to what other people call bad luck; but the bad luck happens far too often for it to be due to chance, so are they 'tapping into' the negative aspects of a collective unconscious? You get what you expect!!

▼─────────────────────────────

*There is plenty to go around—why not
have some for yourself?*

─────────────────────────────▼

# CHAPTER 8

# Learn To See
# The Opportunity!

Those who believe in lack will tell you that 'you only get one chance in life'. One advantage of a lack of education is that no-one told me that. I lived in blissful ignorance so I didn't know that I couldn't become a success several times!

You see, there is no lack. Just look at the abundance all around you. If you look for them, there are chances coming your way all the time! All you need are the attitude, the personal motivation and the eyes to see, and they are yours. If you miss today's opportunity don't worry—there will be another one tomorrow. But, before you *can* see the opportunities, you must be *ready* to see them.

> *An American magazine started a fun column called 'Why Don't They?' and invited its readers to send in suggestions for clever marketing ideas. It started as a few letters; then it grew to a column; it expanded again to a page and finally finished up as a magazine in its own right.*

Here is proof, if you needed it, that there is a massive abundance of opportunity for those who reach out for it. Unfortunately, so many people wait around for someone else to provide it.

As we invent more things, this opens up ever more opportunities to invent yet more things. The can opener would never have been invented, had it not been for the tin can.

All too often, we see the idea when someone else has already achieved it. Then we say, 'That was obvious'. If it was that obvious, why didn't we see it? We only try to do things when someone else has already done it.

### The power of Visualisation

Few people tried to break the four-minute mile before it was broken but, when it was broken, every miler wanted to break it. On his own admission, Roger Bannister was no better than a whole host of other milers around. So what was the difference, if it wasn't ability? He saw the opportunity to be the first.

He had developed the power of **Visualisation** and belief. He could see something which others could not. Yet he had no special gift. Many other milers could have broken that barrier *just by having the vision to see it*. Indeed, once the mental barrier was broken, several other athletes ran under four minutes in the next twelve months. We can all visualise opportunities if we want to. But the definition of vision is looking forward, not back, and most of us look back.

Why, each time I failed, did I just carry on to the next success? *Because I saw opportunity in failure*. I saw opportunity in failure because I was looking forward, and the only way you can look forward is by visualisation.

When most people perceive that they are failing, they are unable to see the way out because they are looking backwards—at what went wrong, what they are going to say to people, how they are going to cope financially or with the loss of a house, how they are going to live with a damaged ego, and so on. But the *only* way out is to look ahead and the only solution is to look for the next opportunity—now!

---

*Once you learn to look forward, once you stimulate your imagination by visualisation, you will see abundant opportunities every day!*

---

### The opportunities are all around you – if you can only see them!

I am not talking about new opportunities outside your normal life but about the opportunities you cannot see which are already there! Opportunities abound to improve or expand your normal life. Vivienne and I have our lovely house only because, when we had nothing, not even a car, I saw this house and said, 'We are going to have that!'

'But it's £350,000!,' she said.

'So what?' I replied. I had seen the house I wanted and, more importantly, because I was broke and about to be evicted, I had seen the positive opportunity to buy it without having to sell one first! But I could only do that because I was looking forward. Had I looked back, I would have seen... nothing, except what I had lost.

From being bankrupt, it took us only eighteen months to buy that house. I can't pretend that we made that much money so quickly. Instead I went to see a mortgage broker.

'A bankrupt wanting a mortgage? No chance!' he said. I thought I was entitled to a second opinion. The second opinion said the same thing. My friends told me not to waste my time. 'It is impossible for a bankrupt to get a mortgage,' they said. Finally, after visiting eighteen brokers, I found one who would agree. I paid through the nose on interest rates, but I got it. You see, I do not look backwards. Had I done so, I would have seen seventeen brokers saying, 'No way!' But opportunity lies in the future and that is where the eighteenth broker was.

As you can imagine, that house means an awful lot to us. It's called 'The Willow'. We get a kick every time we pull into the drive because we got it by refusing to accept the rule of life that, if you are down, you stay down. That was not an option for us. People cannot hold you down if you refuse to stay down; people cannot make you march to the sound of their drums if you are beating your own.

### Look back only to learn

Although the opportunities are there all the time, your ability to see them and take advantage of them will improve with your age and experience of life, provided that you learn to look forward. The opportunities you want to appear will also change as your ambitions, present circumstances and attitudes to life change.

Look back only to learn because the past cannot be changed. What can be changed lies *ahead*, so that is where you must concentrate. As the Bible says, 'Your old men shall dream dreams, and your young men see visions.'* Age does not make people old; if you live in the past, you are old but if you are making plans then you are young.

---

*Joel 2:28.

So is being 'in the right place at the right time' a question of luck? Now you know. The truth is that all of us are *always* in the right place at the right time provided that we believe in the Law of Abundance and provided that we look to the future, not the past. Do that, and you will have the eyes to see the abundant opportunities around you.

▼───────────────────────────────

*Become a child again and have a short memory but big plans*

───────────────────────────────▼

# CHAPTER 9

# You Do Have Choices!

> *The ability to make choices is the single most powerful tool we are given. It is a power unique to Humankind*

Once we accept the Law of Abundance, we must also accept that we have choices because the Law of Abundance is totally meaningless without choice. I do not think that our Creator would create such abundance and then limit our choices as to how we enjoy it. Once we accept that we can make choices, we must also accept that the course of our own life is going to depend on the choices we make.

Therefore, whether we share in the abundance all around us or whether we accept the opposite in life will depend on the choices we make. Your life today is what you chose yesterday. Your life now is the sum total of all the choices you have made in the past. Your life tomorrow is what you will choose today. You may say, 'Sorry, I can't do that because I have got to take the car in for a service.' Well, only because you *choose* to do so. You may say, 'I can't do that because I have family commitments.' Sorry. You are not doing that only because you *choose* to favour the family commitments.

## You have the right to choose—exercise it!

But the ability to make meaningful choices comes only with enough knowledge and experience of life. While we are under parental guidance, we have to allow our parents to make most of our choices for us because we simply do not have enough understanding of the world to make choices for ourselves. Therefore, realistically, the freedom to make totally free choices often becomes relevant only after we have left the parental home. However, there is nothing to stop people choosing when to leave.

Even after that, there are many people who are happy to let someone else make their choices for them. They are *happy* inside with the choices that person makes for them. There is nothing wrong with that.

Many of you, however, are doing what other people expect of you even though that makes you *unhappy* inside. I'm not in the business of breaking up personal relationships but, if you are in that position, make a positive choice now: either decide that someone else does not have the right to be happy at your expense and do something about it, or decide that you are going to accept the present situation and make the best of it. What you cannot do is nothing and then blame the other person for your unhappiness.

I knew a woman who felt that her husband stood self-ishly in the way of her ambitions. So she put these options to him:

'**1.** Either I change,

**2.** Or you change,

**3.** Or we part.

...And *I* do not have the time to change!'

People, particularly spouses or partners in life, relatives or employers, use guilt as a weapon. They make you feel guilty if you do not do what they want—usually by accusing you of selfishness. But remember this:

▼────────────────────────────────────

*If you are not being selfish, you are allowing someone else to be*

────────────────────────────────────▼

If you make the choices other people want you to make (which is the same thing as letting other people make your choices for you), then you cannot blame them if you lose out.

These are strong statements but that does not make them any less true. If success matters enough to you, then you have no option but to accept that:

▼────────────────────────────────────

*Making choices based on what other people want you to do will never make* **you** *successful*

────────────────────────────────────▼

That is one of the most fundamental statements in this book. So, if you want to be successful, make the choices *you* want for yourself.

Choosing means making a definite decision to either *do* or *not do* something. Therefore:

*Wishing* is not choosing.

*Expecting* is not choosing.

*Hoping* is not choosing.

Wishing, expecting or hoping are not choices, they are merely dreams of desired outcomes. They are what you would like to happen as the result of making a choice. But you cannot guarantee that the outcome will be what you wished, expected or hoped for.

### Don't be afraid to make mistakes

So, although the responsibility of making a choice is yours, the *consequences* of making that choice are not your responsibility. Outcomes or consequences are the result of the Law of Cause and Effect.

Having said that, obviously the right outcome can only be a result of making the right choice. But:

▼───────────────────────────

*Unless you make a choice, you cannot have an outcome*

───────────────────────────▼

So don't agonise over making choices—just make them. As I have already said, the world belongs to those who *act*, not to those who only wish, expect or hope. Until you have made a choice and acted on it, you cannot see if you are going to get the right outcome.

If you get the outcome you want, what a good thing you spent no more time agonising over it! But, if you get the wrong outcome, then you have already narrowed the field of possible choices. Move straight on to the next choice and see if that works.

I told you the story of how, even though bankrupt, I still managed to get a mortgage. I chose seventeen wrong mortgage brokers before finding the eighteenth right broker. Had I not been prepared to make seventeen wrong choices, I would never have got a mortgage. Equally, had I spent weeks agonising before making the decision to approach the mortgage brokers, on the basis that 'bankrupts don't get mortgages', then it would have taken me weeks longer to get that mortgage and the house might have been sold in the meantime.

We are taught to be afraid of making choices. We are taught that it is better to avoid action than to make a risky choice. Managers are not judged on all the good choices they make, they are judged by the one bad choice. They use exactly the same yardstick in rating their employees.

Is it any wonder that people think the best way to get on is to follow the adage, 'Keep your nose clean! If there is a problem, make sure you don't get involved! Never volunteer! It does not matter what catastrophe you cause, so long as you can prove that you stuck to the rule-book, you will be O.K.' Bureaucrats are actually told this. Now can you understand why, whenever they are presented with anything out of the ordinary, they are totally unable to use wisdom or common sense—or even a sense of humanity? It has become internalised that 'success' means how well they can follow the rule-book, typified by such sayings as, 'There is no such thing as Justice—only the Law' or, 'I'm only following the rules' or, 'I'm only carrying out instructions' or, 'It's always been done that way.'

You can see that, contrary to popular belief, things start to go wrong when choices are *not* made. So don't be frightened of making the wrong choice *provided* you recognise that, if it proves to be the wrong choice, you just change it! Worry instead about *not* making choices. The only way this philosophy can go wrong is if you let ego make you stick to a wrong choice. If a choice is wrong, you can change it just as easily as you made the first choice. It's no big deal.

## Winners are those who make their own choices

In fact, it is the people who do make choices who become the leaders. Airline pilots make choices but their co-pilots don't; they only obey. If someone stays for too long as a co-pilot, this can become a habit and they may make a bad pilot because they have lost the ability to make choices.

Letting others make decisions for you takes away your power of choice. Athletes who rely too heavily on coaches will lose the ability to make choices; so will people who rely too heavily on a guru; so will workers who rely too heavily on managers. This happened to one of my clients. He was leading a professional golf tournament over-night but his game collapsed the next day because, on his own admission, he had not been able to contact me in the interim!

Not making full and free choices can become a habit with serious consequences, not just on the individual but for society as a whole.

Why was Hitler so successful? Because people saw him as a guru and allowed him to make their choices for them. Having done that, they were unable to take back their ability to make choices. Personal freedom *is* exercising your power of choice. Let other people make your choices for you and you are limiting your personal freedom.

## Choosing means committing to action!

Once we make a choice, then we prepare mentally for the outcome. We are already creating the ability to act. Once actions start, outcomes follow. But, if we have not yet made a choice, our activities are still focused on the choice. Nothing is happening and, because nothing is happening, either there will be no outcome or the outcome will be one we did not choose—or, worse, did not want.

Before you make your choices, you will need to know three things:

***Who else is affected?*** If other people are going to be affected by your desired choice or outcome, they need to know about it! You may need their co-operation and people resist change unless they are consulted. If you are seeking a business outcome then, if at first you cannot get the co-operation you need to succeed, find other people who will co-operate.

Equally, we should not make choices which harm other people. If your choice involves that, *change your choice*.

***What else do I need to know?*** It is a mark of wisdom to collect the information you need in order to make a wise choice. But do not let this become an excuse for delay; balance the need for information against the need to make a choice. As we said before, you cannot look to the outcome until a choice is made so, once you have the information you really need, the sooner you make the choice the better. Taking too long because you are gathering unnecessary information is a form of prevarication. This leads onto:

***By when do I have to make the choice?*** If nothing is achieved by making a choice before a certain date, then don't. *First*, circumstances may change between now and then, so you will have wasted valuable time because you will now have to make a new choice. *Second*, once a choice is made, inertia sets in and people will be loathe to change it even though circumstances now require it. *Third*, new information may appear in the meantime, resulting in a better choice being made. *The best choice you make will often be the one made at the last minute*. My 'gut feeling' has won many more battles than my academic studies ever did!

> *During the French Revolution, it was the policy of the regime to execute every aristocrat they could find.*
>
> *The story goes that one aristocrat chose not to die. He knew that the president of the court had a favourite horse so, when he came before the president, he said, 'If you spare me, I will teach your horse to talk.'*
>
> *The president did not know what to do. If the man was lying, the president would be made a laughing stock. But what if the man could do this? A talking horse! Would he not be the envy of every man in France?*
>
> *'How long will you need?' he asked the aristocrat.*
>
> *'One year,' was the reply.*
>
> *'Then you will have one year,' the president decreed. 'But if, at the end of that time, my horse is not talking, you will be executed.'*
>
> *The gaoler was intrigued by what the aristocrat had done. On the way down to the cells, he could not resist asking, 'But what do you hope to gain by this? Surely you know that you cannot make the horse talk? Surely you know that, in one year, you will be executed anyway?'*

*'Ah!' replied the aristocrat. 'In one year, the president may die. In one year, I may die. But in one year, the horse may talk!'*

The aristocrat was not going to allow anyone else to take his power of choice away from him without a fight. You see, *no-one* can take this power from you. You can, however, give it away or let it be taken away from you. But that is *your* choice.

When, and only when, you have learnt the power of choice, will you be able to take charge of your own life!

### How can you make the best use of your power of choice to create the maximum success for yourself?

If you want to live a well-rounded life, achieving success in all the different areas under your control (personal, physical, mental, spiritual, social and career), then you should exercise your choices with that result in mind. If this is your aim, you will accomplish it by remembering:

▼────────────────────────────────
*Life gives back what we put out*
────────────────────────────────▼

If you want friends, be friendly. If you want understanding, understand others. If you want respect, respect others. If you want love, love others.

Many people who have achieved material success are lonely because they have exercised their choice to achieve only one or two aims: wealth and, perhaps, power. They are people who have exploited others (often their own families) to create their own wealth and that is not going to make them loveable creatures!

Had they started out by asking themselves 'What do I *really* want?' they might have chosen to live by different priorities.

We create our results by the choices we make. If you understand the power of choice then you are enabled to choose your own future. If your present position in life is the result of your past choices, it stands to reason that your future position will depend on your present choices.

But there are certain things you cannot choose. For instance, you cannot choose to end a war or to eliminate crime, because you can only choose to change what you are directly responsible for—and the only thing for which you are responsible is YOU! *If you want to put the world right, put yourself right first.*

However, the results of changing YOU can have side effects and whether these are the effects you want will depend, as we said earlier, on the Law of Cause and Effect. Remember what we said: you cannot determine the outcome, you can only determine the choice you wish to make.

If you make the right choice then you will have the right outcome. But, if you make the wrong choice, choose again! A bad period in your life is usually the result of a choice which, even when it becomes apparent was a bad one, is not changed. This is often caused by not wanting to be seen to be wrong and that is ego.

If you want to share freely in all the abundance and opportunity around you, make up your mind *today* that you are going to choose your *own* future!

# CHAPTER 10

# What Is Success?

Animals eat, sleep and reproduce. Man, unlike animals, strives to improve his environment. He demands more—much more—than the animals. That 'more' is called success.

Ever since the dawn of time, when Man first questioned his relationship with the universe, he has pondered upon the question why, under exactly the same circumstances, one person will succeed but another will fail. The earliest writings of philosophers record arguments and debates on what the actual ingredients of success might be. To this day, writers, debaters, philosophers, psychologists and motivational teachers disagree, in the process not only contradicting one another but often themselves! No-one has yet found a simple answer. That is as it should be because there isn't one!

***Is it action that creates success?*** Some say that people of action have succeeded, suggesting that action is the key. As I have already emphasised, they are correct in assuming that outstanding people are people of action, but they are wrong in assuming that action alone makes success. Action of itself is not a cause, it is an effect. If someone wants to do something, they will act. If they want to do something strongly enough, they will put massive action into achieving it. If they want it with a deep, burning passion, that will result in unstoppable action!

But, what if that action is against the *true* interests of society? Having achieved an aim to the detriment of society, could they be called a success? I think not. Countless human dynamos have wrought massive action on the world, but their only legacy has been human misery or environmental degradation on a large scale. Both Hitler and Robert Maxwell were human dynamos but would you describe either of them as a success?

So action alone is no guarantee of success.

***Does personality create success?*** Other people have been impressed by a person's personality, by their ability to get along with other people. Surely that must be a cause of success? Well, you probably know from your own experience 'nice' people who never seem to get to the top. They leave undisturbed the waters of life. Some of the biggest commercial successes are notoriously disliked. That is not to say that they would not have been more successful had they been more likeable, but their nice personality will not *create* success, it will only add to it.

So personality is not the key.

Nor is success to be found in education, birthright or a high IQ. Just look around you: many successful people have few, if any, of these qualities. In fact, many of these attributes can actually get in the way of success because people who have developed a talent or skill, or have inherited advantages, may attempt to rely on these rather than on their own actions, in pursuit of success—and then wonder why they cannot make it.

Why is it that success sometimes seems to come to those who 'haven't' rather than those who 'have'? I once played golf with Douglas Bader DSO, DFC, the celebrated World War Two fighter pilot who, despite having lost both his legs in air crashes, continued to fly and took up golf! Now, there is a theory in golf which says that the power in a golf swing is developed by leg action. He was unaware of this so, despite having no legs, he consistently hit the ball further than I could! How many people can you think of who have overcome one handicap by creating skill in another way?

A 'where are they now?' survey was done several years ago on the head boys of public schools, to see how well they had done in later life. If it was anyone's birthright to succeed, wouldn't you expect it to be the head boy of a public school? In fact the survey proved that most of them had extremely undistinguished careers.

Social attitudes do not help. We are constantly told, 'You must have education. You cannot get ahead without qualifications.' We have a fixation with intelligence and education. Recruitment counsellors and so-called career-guidance experts are no better; they have persuaded employers that people must pass IQ or aptitude tests. I have yet to meet a successful person where their lack of intelligence, education, the ability to pass an aptitude test or even their lack of the 'gift of the gab' mattered a damn. When I first took up sales, my poor spelling and grammar used to concern me until my boss put my mind at rest. 'While you are selling, I'll do the spelling,' he used to say. Don't get me wrong; I have always regretted my lack of education but, *when it comes to* **creating** *success, my lack of education has never been a problem.*[*]

---

[*] I should add that nor should people be restricted by having a good education. There is no correlation either way between one's standard of education and one's success in life.

The other thing I should explain is that, while people who want to get to the top do not need any of these qualities, *they may need people with these qualities to back them up*. If you want a good accountant in your business, they must have the necessary training and experience. If you want a good PR person, they must have a nice personality and a good background also helps. If you want a good salesperson, they must be willing to act. A good computer programmer needs a high IQ... and so on. But, if *you* want to get to the top, you need none of these things.

A friend of mine told me a story of a millionaire entrepreneur who was thrown out of school in his early teens and never learnt to read. When he was asked if this had ever held him back in life, he said: 'Why would I need to read—I pay people to do that for me!'

Of course, if you already have the attitude and level of personal development you need to succeed, then any other qualities you have may help you to become more successful. But you cannot rely on them to get you to the top *in place of* attitude and personal development; they can only *add to* attitude and personal development.

### The true key to success

This leads us to the key to success:

▼————————————————————————

*Success is more what a person is, rather than what they do*

————————————————————————▼

All successful people have a certain attitude. They see themselves as winners. They see themselves as achievers. Now, that is very easy to do once you have won, once you have achieved! But what really sets them apart from other people is that *they saw themselves as winners before they had even started; they saw themselves as achievers before they had even started!* They did not ask, 'What if I lose?', they concentrated on winning.

Although people take comfort in saying of successful people, 'They were lucky' or, 'They were in the right place at the right time' (the inference of course being that, if *I* had been in that place at that time, I, too, would have been successful; or that success is due to luck and I have been unlucky), the opposite is in fact true. *Successful people achieve success by planning, not by accident.*

There is no such thing as 'being in the right place at the right time'. Instead, I will show you how to create the right time wherever you are and you, too, will learn how to get lucky because creating luck is no more than creating the right attitude.

> *Gary Player, the golfer, was considered to be the greatest bunker-player of his day. When a reporter referred to him as being the luckiest bunker-player around, Gary retorted: 'The more I practice, the luckier I seem to get!'*

People who are not yet successful may assume that success comes from doing the unusual, so they look for something unusual to do. Now, I am not saying that people have not become successful by doing the unusual but *the vast majority of people have become successful by doing ordinary things extraordinarily well.*

Richard Branson did not invent airlines; nor did he invent records. Alan Sugar was well-known for using out-dated technology, yet he took his company (Amstrad) to the top in an incredibly fast time. It is much easier to achieve success that way simply because there are more abundant opportunities to do ordinary things extraordinarily well than there are to find unusual things to do.

Let me give you an example: most sports people reach the top by doing the same things as other people, but better. Linford Christie, Mohammed Ali, Sebastian Coe, Jimmy Connors, Ian Botham, Stanley Matthews, Jack Nicklaus, Chris Bonnington and, just recently, Brian Lara, all did ordinary things extraordinarily well. But how many sports people can you think of who got to the top by doing the unusual? Dick Fosbury invented the Fosbury Flop in high jumping and broke the world record. But he did not stay there for long because the Fosbury Flop soon become the ordinary, and other people soon did it better than he.

Although I have used sportspeople as examples because it is easier to illustrate the point, if you are looking for commercial success or success in personal relationships or simply trying to get out of financial hardship, there are two major differences between you and a sportsperson: first, to get to the top, sportspeople have to have skill to support both their attitude and level of personal motivation; and, second, their level of personal motivation usually results in a total dedication to their chosen sport to the exclusion of other areas in their lives. But the road to success in the commercial and personal fields is less arduous and *we all have the basic talents we need, provided we develop the right attitude and level of personal motivation*.

## How to measure your own success

But what does success actually consist of?

Some people think that success is a matter of comparison with others. That is not success. Depending on where a person is coming from, that is Greed ('I want what they have got'), Power ('I want to have more than they have got'), or Low Self-esteem ('I need what they have got to prove that I am as good as they are').

Genuine success is not a matter of comparison. Genuine success is what we do with our own potential. It is whether you get what you want for yourself, not what you want because other people have got it or because someone else wants you to get it.

Success is therefore achieving a particular goal. In fact, in the words of Paul J. Meyer:

▼――――――――――――――――――――――

*'Success is the progressive realisation of a worthwhile, pre-determined, personal goal'*

――――――――――――――――――――――▼

*Progressive* means that you must be constantly setting more personal goals. If you stop doing this, you are no longer being successful. You *were* successful but you are no longer.

This goes back to what I said earlier, that Man, left to his natural state, is a striver. Once he stops striving, once he stops having a purpose in life, he starts to lose his life force. Therefore, success has to be related to your true potential. If it is not worthwhile, if it is not in some way extending you, it is not releasing your potential. This means that success is related to things which you have not yet done. It is not, as many people believe, a comparison with what others have done, nor is it related to what you have *already* done.

In my own business life, my goal was to build up my financial resources to be able to do what I really wanted to do—which is what I am doing now!—passing onto others the secrets of how to release their own true potential. The journey has involved seeking to do things which I hadn't done before and which I knew would extend me—like this book project.

If I had no goal in sight, how would I have known what to do next?

Most people when they look for success are too vague, too broad in their definition of what they want. Too often, they try to define their wants as wealth. But wealth *of itself* is not success. If people want wealth *for its own sake*, they either have low self-esteem and need wealth to prove to themselves that they are as good as others, or they have a fear of insecurity and see wealth as a form of barrier against poverty. The sad thing about both categories is that they never actually achieve success in their own eyes! If you want wealth to show other people that you are as good as they are, there is always going to be someone wealthier than you—and therefore, in your eyes, a more worthwhile human being than you.

It is sad not to be able to enjoy wealth; people with the constant need to have more than someone else suffer the same way as the old gunslingers of the West: there is always someone around who wants to outshoot them.

If a person accumulates wealth because they see it as a hedge against insecurity, they also suffer constant fear:

'What happens if I lose my millions?' 'There could be a massive devaluation.' 'The world markets could collapse.' It is actually impossible to accumulate enough wealth to get rid of these fears!

The only value in wealth is that it allows you to purchase the sort of lifestyle you want for yourself. Success is what you are, not what you've got. Even at the times when I had lost all my wealth, I did not feel a failure because I knew that my success was inside me. A person who feels a failure is not able to look at a £350,000 house and say, 'We are going to have that!' A bankrupt who believes that he is a failure is not going to go to eighteen mortgage brokers to get that house.

Bankruptcy is a material state, but it should not be a mental state. I know millionaires who, despite all their wealth, have bankrupt minds. But I also know people with little money who have minds which are a treasure-trove of wealth. Believe me, it is many times worse to have a bankrupt mind than it is to be materially bankrupt.

People may take everything we have in the outside world but they cannot take away what we have inside, provided that we have an understanding of what success really is.

It is making the journey which is the success and this is why true success is more than the accumulation of wealth.

Having said that, some people find success in doing a job well; others find the success more in the striving than in the achieving; yet others find success not in what they have, but in how they use it.

## How do we achieve success?

▼————————————————————————

- *By having a belief in our own potential*
- *By having a good self-image*
- *By taking personal responsibility for our
  motivation*

————————————————————————▼

Let's examine these more closely:

### Having belief in your human potential

If you want to achieve something, you have to believe that you possess the potential to achieve it. If you do not believe you can achieve it, you have already failed.

This may sound very obvious but I do see many people working, sometimes extremely hard, for something which they do not believe, deep down, that they can actually achieve. This is where the power of the sub-conscious mind comes in: people can convince them-selves that they are going to succeed. They do this by blocking out at the *conscious* level any doubts about success. But these doubts still exist at the *subconscious* level and it is beliefs at the *subconscious* level which really decide the way we act. Belief is belief; there is no compromise.

But it is not enough to believe in the human potential. You must also believe, 'I am entitled to that!' and this is where self-esteem comes in.

### Having a good self-image

All successful people understand the importance of having a good self-image. This is not the same as being conceited or having an inflated ego. It is more a case of having a wholesome respect for oneself, of being proud of oneself.

Too many people stop any chance of success by having a low self-image.

The Japanese specialise in the art of bonsai. They create dwarf trees by continuously cropping the roots so that the tree is never allowed to grow. People with low self-esteem have had their 'roots cropped' in the same way. There is even an expression for it: they are constantly 'cut down to size' by people who have strong influence over them—parents, teachers, brothers, sisters, loved ones, employers and so on.

Low self-esteem shows itself in doubt that the person can achieve and a belief that, even if they do, they are not entitled to it. It follows that a person with low self-esteem will never reach too far.

> *A man in one of the Southern States of America made his living by selling helium-filled balloons of many colours, at fairgrounds. When he set up his pitch, he used to release some of these into the air to attract children. One day, he was approached by a little black boy.*
>
> *'Please sir,' the child asked, 'can you tell me how high the black balloon will go?'*
>
> *'Why, child,' the balloon seller replied, understanding what was behind the boy's question, 'they are all filled with the same amount of gas, so it is what is on the inside which makes them go up, no matter what the colour.'*

Because a person *feels* inferior does not always mean that they will *act* inferior—again, the reverse is often the case. As we said before, people of low self-image do set out to become wealthy in the mistaken belief that this will prove they are as good as anyone else.

So low self-esteem need not limit the accumulation of wealth (I am not going to call that success because it is done for the wrong reasons). Indeed, in this case, it was the reason for it. It does, however, stop personal development.

One reason for low self-esteem is that we are taught that self-love is wrong. The origin of this is based in faulty religious instruction misunderstanding the true meanings of humility and selfishness. The fact is that no philosophy in the world, including *properly* taught religious philosophies, teaches us not to love ourselves. If religious instructors were to read the Bible properly, they would see that it says, 'Love thy neighbour *as* yourself.'* Not more than; not instead of; but *as*.

Parents and teachers also cause much low self-esteem with such statements as, 'Don't be so smart!' or, 'You can't have everything!' and, 'Children should be seen and not heard!'

Society, too, plays a major part in lowering people's self-esteem. If a person has a more 'junior' position than someone else, they are labelled as 'less important'. People who are less clever or poorly educated are labelled as 'worse' than others who are lucky enough to have these advantages. In the UK, someone who comes from a 'lower' class is adjudged as 'inferior'; someone who has very little, but has worked for everything they have got, is seen as lower in status than someone who has inherited wealth and not done a day's work for it. If ever you needed proof that success

---

*Matthew 19:19.

is not wealth, I rest my case right here. So deeply rooted in society are these notions of worth that the courts vary the severity of their sentences according to the defendant's class, as if it is less of an offence when committed by someone of a higher class. We have to learn to be bigger than the system.

The fact is that you do not need an excuse to live in the world you were born to enjoy, so how do we improve our self-image? You will find that this is one of the threads running through this book.

Do not underestimate your importance in this world. We all have the capacity to contribute no matter in how 'small' a way. It is what we do with what we've got which measures our status, so we must start to see ourselves with new eyes. You are a valuable human being with the resources to become even more valuable to society.

> *Since the beginning of civilisation, the penicillin mould was seen as a nuisance with no known value or use. No-one was able to recognise it, yet all its potential was already there! Its value only came when we learnt how to use it.*

This is exactly the same as self-image: its importance only becomes obvious when we learn to use it.

You must also learn to act with as much dignity to yourself as you would to other people. Would you call anyone else silly, stupid, slow? Well, don't call yourself that! Learn to treat yourself as your best friend because that, indeed, is just what you are! You are the only person guaranteed to be with you for life! If you have high self-esteem you will value yourself just as much as anyone else.

I have seen professional golfers whose reaction to a bad shot is to admonish themselves: 'You stupid...!' But do they react the same way to their best friend or partner playing a bad shot? No. They understand that the best way to help someone follow a bad shot with a good one is to encourage not demean them, so they are more likely to say something like, 'Don't worry—you always play a great shot to get out of trouble.' Don't treat yourself more harshly than you would your best friend—admonishing yourself is just as bad as admonishing them!

It is not just in your outward actions to yourself that you should treat yourself with pride; think of yourself with pride, too.

***Don't doubt yourself! You've got this far, so why not go further?*** If you get self-doubt, learn to counteract it with pride in yourself. Say,

'I can—because...
'I am—because...
'I will—because...
'I CAN!!'

As a test of your self-image, write down all the things you dislike about yourself. When you look closely, you will find that much of what you dislike is not really as bad as you imagined. Then list everything you like about yourself. It is a good idea to get your family and friends involved in just the *second* part of this exercise. For a good self-image, it is important that *you* like 'you'. You are probably a better person than you thought!

### Taking personal responsibility for our motivation

The whole theme of this book is that success comes to those who accept, and take, *personal* responsibility for their own lives by accepting:

> *'I am responsible for where I am now (not my partner in life, my boss, society, the government, my parents or anyone else).'*

> *'I am responsible for getting to where I want to be.'*

> *'I am responsible for the choices I make in life.'*

If anyone is not prepared to accept *total* responsibility for each of the above, if anyone chooses to lay any blame elsewhere for any part of their lack of success, they cannot achieve their aims.

# CHAPTER 11

# What Stops Success?

If everyone is capable of creating the self-motivation to act but they are not doing so then, clearly, they need to change something.

Old-school psychologists will have you believe that habits of thinking are entrenched at an early age, so they cannot be changed. Neither the assumption nor the conclusion is true, and this been proved time and time again. Habits *can* be changed. Therefore, even if a person is not personally motivated at present, they can *learn* to be—and then they *will* be!

If we have unlimited potential, the power to be self-motivated and the power of choice to allow ourselves to take full advantage of a world overflowing with abundance and opportunity, *why are we not all successful people*? If a new born baby has every ingredient to be successful, why are so many people leading lives of mediocrity by middle age? What stopped their success?

I have found many reasons for people's inability to succeed, but they all come under four headings:

- Putting things off.
- Complacency
- No Goals
- Loss of Desire.

## Putting things off, or Procrastination

Procrastination is not doing what you know you should do. Most people procrastinate because they feel it is not urgent to them. The trouble is that it does become urgent, but only when it is too late! The future has a nasty habit of picking up on the very things you did *not* do!

When a procrastinator sees it is too late, they lose some of their self-belief because they know that they should have acted, but didn't. As a result, they feel guilty. You would think that the guilt feeling alone would lead them to act the next time that same situation arises, but in fact it has the opposite effect: from then on, they actually doubt their ability to deal with that state of affairs.

Successful people are required to do exactly the same tasks as procrastinators. So the best answer is to develop a sense of urgency about your work—a 'do it now' attitude; do it now and do it properly.

▼────────────────────────────────────────

*Successful people do ordinary things extraordinarily well*

────────────────────────────────────────▼

...And they bring a sense of *urgency* to their tasks.

## Complacency

Complacency is sometimes a Procrastinator without a Conscience—they don't do it and they don't care that they aren't doing it because they feel that it is someone else's responsibility: 'It's not my job to do it because I am the manager!' or, 'It's not my job to do it because I am *not* the manager!'

Complacent people can also be bored people. They've done it before and they are not looking forward to doing it again.

So far, we have looked at people who are not succeeding. However, complacent people can be people who have succeeded but have set no new goals for themselves. They've 'made it' and they are not about to 'make it' again by doing something else.

Complacency often follows on from procrastination. If a person does not learn to *act* instead of procrastinating, they will in the end get tired of feeling guilty about it. The result is to convince themselves that 'It doesn't matter. And who cares anyway?'

Complacent people surrender to an inner urge to take it easy. They look for the easy things to do and they seek the easy ways out. One of their tricks is always to have something else to do which does not extend them.

Complacent people are often not being deliberately so; it is easy to genuinely convince oneself that what one is doing is important, whereas the real reason for doing it is to avoid having to tackle a harder or more unpleasant task. To avoid this, remember that *winners do what losers won't*.

At its extreme, complacency can show itself in a convenient dose of 'flu, rather than having to face an unpleasant situation at work. Even the victim may not be aware of what is happening and may be absolutely convinced that they are genuinely ill; however, those who have the motivation to get things done will do so despite illness, just as Vivienne did in the face of cancer.*

A lack of personal belief can cause both complacency and procrastination. A person may doubt their ability to handle a given situation. The result is that they won't try to deal with it because they are frightened of failing, so they cover-up with statements like, 'It's not worth it' or, 'It will sort itself out'.

But complacency can cause a more sinister problem. If a person is not performing to the best of their ability, they obviously risk getting found out. The best way to avoid that is to drag everyone else down to their level by making sure that *they* are not doing their job right, either. Or, they may actually resent other people succeeding where they are failing. Either way, their solution is to distract their workmates as much as possible. How often have you heard someone say, 'I would not take the manager's job even if they offered it to me.' Are these not the people who spend their day finding fault with the system rather than trying to improve it?

It is one of the laws of Nature that everything grows, levels off then dies. Every plant, every animal, even buildings, grow, level off and die.

Complacency is the levelling-off stage because the person no longer wants to make the effort to grow. 'Being in a rut' is a definition of complacency; the trouble is that the only difference between a rut and a grave is the depth; some say that a rut *is* a grave with the ends kicked out.

Complacent people, if they are lucky, will find a safe harbour and hide there. If *you* are moored up in the

---

*See page 15.

harbour of complacency, pull up your anchor and head out to sea. *You* are the captain of your ship *and there are new lands to discover!*

## No Goals

Here is someone else staying in their comfort zone, standing still, going nowhere. People with no goals are not prepared to do what winners do because they do not feel that it is worth it.

The sad thing about people without goal-drive is that it very often takes no more effort to aim high than it does to aim low. People rarely achieve more than they set out to achieve.

People without goals often want success but they are not prepared to pay the price. Everyone wants to go to heaven but nobody wants to *die*. No winner can afford to wait until they 'feel like it'. They are prepared to pay the price of giving up doing things they hold dear, working long hours, making themselves unpopular, being out in all weathers—*whatever needs to be done, they do it.*

People without goals do not realise that the world of success extracts an entry fee from achievers; they want success but do not feel that it is necessary to pay the price. They think that the world of success owes them and then do not understand when the world of success does not agree. The world of success decides the rules and they are not up for discussion. People who set low goals think that they can change the rules but they cannot, so they turn to excuses.

Low goal-setters need to learn to become self-starters. They need to develop the sense of urgency to do it now. They need to understand that anything is possible. Even if they have not got there yet, that is no reason to settle for being less than they can be.

The way to do this may be for them to reset their goals because the goals they have now may not be stretching them. If they do not believe that their goals are worth the effort, THEY ARE PROBABLY RIGHT!

People without goals are often controlled by outside influences. They may well want to succeed but they cannot make the commitment because, 'He or she will not let me!' This, of course, is another form of not being prepared to pay the price, but more understandably so. People too often have to choose between their ambitions and their relationships and that is not a decision anyone should have to make. If you find yourself in this position, then it is time to talk with your partner!

However, if you develop a strong Inner Force, that force will always be stronger than any outside influences.

### The Great Demotivators

*A farmer wanted to borrow a tractor from a neighbour who lived three fields away.*

*It was dark as he set off across the fields. But then, as he walked, he began to wonder if it was worth the trip.*

*'I'll bet it's low on fuel,' he thought. 'That means that I am going to have to drive the tractor to town to fill the tank up.*

*'So I'll need the lights. There's bound to be a problem with those. I'll need to get the mechanic to come out*

*and fix them—and I expect he won't be prepared to come out this late.*

*'Anyway, he's bound to want his tractor back for the morning because he's sure to need it himself.'*

*He got to the neighbour's house and rang the bell. As he waited for the neighbour to unlock the door, another thought occurred to him, '...And I bet the damned thing breaks down on the way back!'*

*Just then, the neighbour, opened the door. 'Yes?' he said.*

*'You know just where you can stick your tractor!' the farmer replied.*

He saw failure before he started!

The great demotivators are fear, doubt and worry. In fact, worry and doubt are only degrees of fear: if you have no fear of something, you would not worry about it and there would be no need to feel doubt about it. Fear of impending failure makes it much easier not to act, than to act and fail.

▼─────────────────────────────

*Most worries never happen, most doubts are unfounded and most fears are groundless*

─────────────────────────────▼

Nevertheless, they take up valuable time and energy by making you focus on the problems rather than on the result. The answer is to keep reminding yourself of why you are doing it.* You must never forget why you want

───────────────

*How you do this is shown on page 122.

it. If your desire is not strong enough, go back to Chapter One and rebuild your belief.

Although there is almost always another chance, a good technique is to convince yourself that this actually is the last one you will get. You must believe that you cannot bail out.

Courage is the right response to fear and the aim of the above two paragraphs is to give you a technique to replace fear with courage.

Another technique is to follow this procedure:

- Appraise the situation both emotionally and logically

- Then form a plan of action

- Then *ACT* on that plan.

Action gets fear into perspective and this should carry you through the fear. Once an unpleasant situation has been dealt with in this way, it should become easier to handle with courage and confidence in the future.

When you develop a conviction in your own potential, when you genuinely believe that all of us (including you) have within us the seeds of our own success, two things will happen: your fear will go because there is no longer anything to fear; and you will stop looking for your salvation in someone or something else, because people only do that if they do not believe that they have the power of their own salvation within themselves.

Once you realise that, your fear will go. Far from the fear of failure preventing you from acting (which is what holds most of us back), you will realise that:

▼─────────────────────────────

### *The failure is in **not** acting*

─────────────────────────────▼

### Loss of desire

Loss of desire causes loss of purpose. Like the previous three, loss of purpose is the result of short-sightedness caused by there being nothing further away to look at. Like the others, your goals are either not appealing enough or you have forgotten them.

There is nothing sadder than someone who sets out to climb a hill and then stops short. That way, they will never see the Promised Land. So the crime is not in failure, it is in not aiming.

*Remember why you started.* Don't let yourself be put off by complacent people; you can spot them by the negative stories they love to tell!

DO IT *NOW!* Reset your goals and go for the stars— *NOW!*

# CHAPTER 12

# Motivation—The Inner Force

- Now that we believe in the *limitless* potential of Man,

- Now that we believe in the Law of Abundance,

- Now that we know that opportunity *abounds* around us,

- Now that we know *we* have the power to choose those opportunities,

- Now that we have *pride* in ourselves,

- Now that we know *'we are entitled to it'*...

...we can look at the final part of the jigsaw—*how to develop and release the power of personal motivation*!

We established* that success is the progressive realisation of worthwhile, predetermined personal goals. The power to actually *achieve* those goals is called personal motivation—The Inner Force.

▼——————————————————————

*There is no way you can achieve your goals unless you first create a high enough level of personal motivation to want to achieve them*

——————————————————————▼

—————————————

\* See page 74.

## But what exactly is motivation?

Well, you can define it in different ways:

- Motivation is the cause of behaviour
- Motivation is the inner urge that impels you to act
- Motivation is a desire strong enough to cause action.

So motivation involves *action* or, more specifically, the creation and continuation of action until the causation, the urge or the desire is satisfied.

The word **MOTIVATION** splits into two words:

MOTIV   ATION

...Making two rather obvious words!:

MOTIVE   ACTION

People need a motive in order to act or, looked at the other way round, people won't act without a motive to do so. So the actual picture is:

**MOTIVE $\Rightarrow$ ACTION**

Put in its simplest terms, a MOTIVE to ACT is a REASON to DO.

But what about the two missing letters: 'E' from motive and 'C' from action? Well, they stand for two things you do *not* want! 'E' stands for Excuses; 'C' stands for Complacency and complacency, as we saw in the last chapter, is one of the reasons for not acting.

It is an impossibility to do anything at all without the *motivation* to do it. The way—the *only* way—it is possible to do anything is to first build up the motivation to do it. If you do not, you will stay put right where you are!

### Make motivation a way of life

Once you start to act, however, then the only difference between success and failure is in the attitude behind your actions. Let me give you an example. Very few people actually *want* to do a bad job; often the reason for doing so is a reaction to bad management. The attitude of someone in this predicament often is, 'Why should I bother to do a good job? My boss doesn't deserve it. Instead, I'll do the worst job I can, just to get my own back on him. Anyway, he never appreciates what I do, so what is the point?' An employee who thinks in this way will end up by hurting themselves more than their manager.

No matter how bad the manager is, won't an employee be much happier if they think, 'If I do a really good job, I will feel very good about myself. Even if my boss does not appreciate me, the customers will. Anyway, I want a pay-rise and promotion and that is the best way to get it'?

The only difference between the first employee and the second is that the thoughts of the first motivate them towards failure; therefore they *cannot* succeed. The thoughts of the second motivate them towards success and therefore they have vastly reduced their chances of failure. The same applies to a parent or to a sportsperson who is competing against superior success stories. Sportspeople in this position must *at least* set the target of beating their personal best otherwise it is too easy to give in to the negative thought, 'I am only here to make up the numbers!'

To make sure you do a job as well as you possibly can, all you have to do is to change your motivation *against* doing a good job to one *for* doing a good job. You do that simply by changing the thought in your head. In other words, you gave yourself a reason *for* good action, not a reason *against* it.

*All successful people have high levels of personal motivation*; some taught themselves (or, to be more accurate, it probably just happened to them!); others have had it bred into them by parents, teachers, employers and their partner in life. More important than that:

▼───────────────────────────

*The habit of successful people is to* **always** *look for reasons to act,* **never** *to look for reasons not to act*

───────────────────────────▼

Therefore what really sets successful people apart from the rest is not only that they have a high level of personal motivation to carry out a specific act,

▼───────────────────────────

*It is that a high level of personal motivation has become a way of life, a reaction to* **everything** *they do, a habit*

───────────────────────────▼

Theoretically, motivation could be done for you. Someone else could carry out the three exercises which are the power behind personal motivation. They could:

- Set your goals for you
- Help you to work towards them, then
- Set your new goals for you.

But that would not make you successful. One can temporarily motivate another *only* if they want to be motivated. The only worthwhile motivation is driven by *personal* desire. Without desire from within, motivation cannot last. That's why I call it the Inner Force.

Very few people understand this. Most managers, most motivational trainers, see motivation as a force which can be applied externally. This is not so; the key to continuing motivation lies inside a person. Someone outside can help that person to find the key to unlock the power of their motivation—their Inner Force—but they cannot *create* it on any long-term basis. Therefore, if a desire does not come from within, the motivation cannot last; only *personal* motivation lasts.

Of course, you can learn self-motivation from others and that is the purpose of this book. But, from there, you need to master the art of self-direction.

*People often get confused between Training and Motivation.* Training teaches you what to do but it is motivation that makes do what you have been taught to do.

If you are a leader, here's a question you should ask yourself: 'If my people actually did everything they had been taught to do, how much extra productivity would I get?' In other words, if you are in sales, how much extra business would you get? If you are in production, how much better would the quality of your products be? If you run an office, how much more, and *better*, work would be done if your staff did what they had been *taught* to do? You see, the answer of almost all managers, when people do not do what they are trained to do, is to give them yet more training. In fact, the problem is almost always that people do not have the personal motivation to do what they are trained to do.

*It is a common belief that all emotions are bad and all logic is good.* This point of view sees emotion and logic as being in conflict with each other but they are not—properly used, they *complement* each other. Both play their part in creating a successful, rounded whole.

Emotions have a serious purpose. Anger and fear are defence mechanisms but, allowed to appear at the wrong times, they are destructive to our own aims. So we need to control our emotions by logic and be certain about what we feel and why we feel that way. If the emotion is counter-productive to our effort, we should control the emotion with logic.

However, that does not make logic more important than emotion. If you want to make love, then logic is the very last thing you need around!

The power of emotion is a significant part of personal motivation—if you apply being *emotive* to *motive*, you will get *action*. If you are emotive enough, you will get massive action. The emotions we are looking for here are enthusiasm, passion and desire.

▼──────────────────────────

### Logic is the enemy of massive success

──────────────────────────▼

*Logic is therefore the enemy of the Inner Force.* The great achievers often do what logic and reason, if they allowed themselves to listen to it, would tell them cannot be done. It is always logic that says, 'It can't be done!' Logic sours dreams; logic stifles creativity; logic denies abundance; logic kills opportunity.

But logic, in its place, is as important as emotion. *However grandiose your scheme, it cannot be achieved without planning.* So conceive your goals in emotion, but plan them with logic. Dream your dreams then plan their achievement.

The bumble-bee has flown for many millions of years. Yet, until very recently, logic and reason told us it was actually incapable of flying—because according to the dynamics of flight as we understood them, its wing area was to small for its body. So technically it should not have been able to fly.

But fly it did. Luckily for the bumble-bee, it did not read books on aeronautics!

# ◀Part III▶

# Realise That Potential!

## Put your ideas into action

# CHAPTER 13

# Habit Is The Lock
# And Attitude Is The Key

How do we turn our personal motivation into success? How do we convert our Inner Force into outward action?

We have to change our present habits into the habits of success. And, to do that, we first have to change our attitude. The habits we have now were first formed as a result of attitude. If you have always hated smoking then you would not have developed the habit of smoking. People develop the smoking habit because of their attitude: how many people can truthfully say that they enjoyed their first cigarette? So perhaps their attitude to peer pressure was stronger than their dislike of smoking (in other words, under pressure from their friends, they did not want to seem the odd-one-out by not smoking); or their parents or people they respected smoked, and therefore their attitude was that it was 'O.K.'; or they copied role models on the screen or in advertisements.

The trouble is that, once the habit is formed, it then starts to reinforce and control your attitude. Despite being aware of the dangers, a smoker will aggressively defend the habit—an example of the habit creating the attitude. From here on, as any person who has tried to give up smoking will testify, it does not matter how much you want to give up smoking, the habit is now actually stronger than the attitude! Therefore habit and attitude form a circle, each reinforcing the other. The attitude first allows the habit to form, which then strengthens the attitude, which then reinforces the habit, which further hardens the attitude, which...

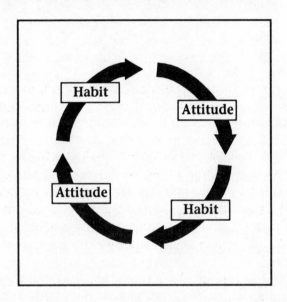

The reason why people find it so difficult to break a habit *even when they really want to* is because they don't understand that you cannot successfully break any habit without changing the attitude first, and *wanting* to change the attitude is not enough. A *reason* to change is needed. People who have heart problems may not find it so difficult to give up smoking because they have now found a strong enough reason to do so. Their attitude to smoking usually becomes hostile as a result.

Many people see habits as bad things. If you say someone has a habit, you are usually referring to a bad habit. 'Doing things as a matter of habit' is meant as a criticism. People with habits are seen as predictable and therefore boring—and certainly this is not a word used when describing successful people.

In fact, this negative attitude towards habits is very far from the truth. Successful people are very much creatures of habit. They find what works for them and then they stick to it as a habit. They work long hours as a habit. They treat people in a habitual way which happens to be the way that brought them success. Self-discipline is a habit with them.

If we did not form habits, we would get far less done in a day. Can you remember what it was like the first time you drove a car? 'How am I supposed to press down with one foot while at the same time lifting the other one up—and now the instructor wants me to indicate (by the way, which way does the indicator stalk go?) *and* look over my shoulder *and* slowly release the handbrake all at the same time?'

A very short while later, you could find yourself driving quite fast, while carrying on a conversation and listening to music at the same time—and all with no difficulty at all.

What has happened is that, by continued practice, your ability to drive has become a habit and, when something becomes a habit, this releases your brain to deal with other matters at the same time.

It is habits which get us through everyday life. You can dress quickly in the morning only because you learnt how to dress the hard way and then gradually got quicker as it became a habit. How long would it take you to get dressed in the morning if you had to work out how to do every single movement? You only have to see the sad picture of someone with senile dementia to realise what happens when the mind can no longer rely on habits to perform even the simplest tasks.

## How to reform your habits

If we understand how habits are formed, we are in a position to consciously *reform* them. So what steps does the mind go through to develop a habit?

1. You experience a situation.

2. The situation requires conscious thought.

3. Based on your attitude to your thoughts, you make a decision.*

4. If the decision has a favourable result, you will put this information into the computer of your mind.

5. Next time you experience that situation, the computer of your mind will look to match it with a similar experience. If it finds one, it will advise you on how to react to that situation.

6. You will now react automatically either physically or mentally to the situation—in other words, by habit.

7. Each time you do this the habit gets stronger until, eventually, the conscious mind does not need to be used at all; it is simply bypassed.

Habits do not differentiate between good decisions and bad ones, they only do what they have been programmed to do. This means that *you* may not recognise a habit as being good or bad. However, you may recognise being unhappy with the *result* of that habit; if you do, and if you feel strongly enough about it, you will use the conscious mind to try find a better solution.

---

*Your thoughts themselves will be coloured by your previous experiences, beliefs and attitudes.

Our attitude is the term we use for how we see things in our mind. Our habits are the action we take, based on how we see things.

As we said earlier, in order to change a habit successfully, you first need to change the attitude which created it. You do this by:

**1.** Recognising the habit for what it is. The purpose of a habit is to achieve some form of satisfaction.

**2.** Knowing the satisfaction that it gives.

**3.** Then substituting the habit with one that gives more satisfaction and doing it repeatedly.

It is not easy to change habits. Habits are formed in order to make life easier or more satisfying. It follows that changing them must be harder than forming them in the first place.

As an example, suppose that you have developed the habit of sleeping late in the morning. Then, following the above formula, we might finish up with:

**1.** Recognising that sleeping late is not tiredness. It is escapism.

**2.** Realising that the satisfaction is from not having to face the day.

**3.** Could you get up early to do something you really liked? Then the answer is to substitute something pleasurable to be achieved over the next few days by getting up early.

If your substitute activity was pleasurable enough, you should find the habit broken and waking up early becomes a habit.

Changing habits can have powerful results. For example:

▼───────────────────────────

*If you were to work for just half-an-hour
more per day, you would create for
yourself a thirteen-month year. Could
**you** achieve more with an extra month?*

───────────────────────────▼

In my experience, one of the most important habits to develop is the habit of setting goals. And it is this habit which we explore in the next chapter.

# CHAPTER 14

# Goals—The Powerhouse

Some of you may have tried goal-setting programmes, only to find they were not successful. I hope it gives you confidence that I, too, have tried other systems without success! In the end, I devised my own and the one I am going to show you now has been successfully used by many people from many different walks of life to achieve many different goals.

The reason why goal-setting has not worked for some people is not because the concept is wrong but because it was poorly applied. Some systems, while recognising the importance of long-term goals, entirely miss the absolutely *vital* necessity of breaking down the achievement of those long-term goals into daily and weekly steps and then, as well as visualising the long-term goals, 'seeing' yourself achieving those daily and weekly steps.

If your goal is to build a boat in three years, it is no good just visualising it and expecting it to happen! In order to achieve that goal, you need to know what bits have got to be put together on a daily and weekly basis.

Goal-setting, like any other skill, needs practice. Set, visualise and practice daily goals for a while and then expand into visualising weekly goals. Only after this is working, should you move to monthly and then yearly goals. The advantage of this system is that, by concentrating on short-term, relatively easy steps, your mind will disregard the doubts that can arise about whether you can achieve those bigger goals.

The first thing to do is to see in which areas of your life you can—and should—set goals. There are six of these areas which, like the segments of an orange combine together to make the whole 'You':

This is called 'The Wheel of Life', with you as the outer rim and the areas of your life as the spokes.

Just like a wheel, your Wheel of Life needs to be properly balanced if your aim is to find the most fulfilled life of which you are capable. If your Wheel of Life gets out of round, then your ride will get rough!

One of the myths of life is that, in order to achieve out-standing success in one part of your life (perhaps aim-ing for the top in business, or becoming a world-beating athlete, a renowned musician or a missionary), you must sacrifice everything else in your life. George Graham, the football manager, believed this. His regret, he said, was that success had meant losing valu-able time with his family. What a price to pay! We can, if we approach our lives in the right way, achieve the success we want without such sacrifice.

So my aim is to help you to become, not just success-ful, but happy as well and that means leading a bal-anced life. You achieve that by setting goals in each area. Let me stress, this does *not* mean that you need to compromise massive success in one area. That is not to say that you may not need temporarily to shelve some goals in some areas; there are not enough hours in the day to attack each area with gusto! So what you need to do is to prioritise your goals but at the same time recognise that *you will need at some stage to balance them up*.

It will pay you to discuss your plans with people who are going to be affected by them, perhaps telling your family before you start, so that they can adjust to the changes in you.

The first thing is to decide what goals you do want. You do that by making out your own plan of the future, '*My Personal Plans*', and I show you how to do this in the final chapter.

Do you remember that, on page 81, I asked you to list the things you do not like about yourself? What about starting to put those right? If there are, for example, twelve things on that list, correcting one a month will create a really good self-image for yourself in a year's time!

I cannot stress enough the importance of starting with immediate, daily goals. You need to learn the system through daily practice before embarking on weekly or monthly goals. Planning a yearly goal at this stage is like asking an eight year old what they want to be when they grow up; the answer can only be based on what they know now when it needs to be based on their knowledge of themselves in the future, once they have developed a more mature understanding.

But goals on their own are not enough. You have to bring them to life through the power of Visualisation. To find out how, turn to the next chapter...

# CHAPTER 15

# Visualisation And The Law Of Attraction

Visualisation is focusing your thoughts into a specific picture. In order to reach success, you must first be able to see it *clearly* in your mind's eye.

One key to my own success is the ability to 'think it through' in logical sequence. Vivienne calls this technique 'becoming a master of consequence'—in other words, learning to 'see' what a certain course of action will lead to.

This mental picturing is what takes wishful thinking into goal accomplishment. If you think of all the world's achievements, *someone saw them before they happened*. The wheel could be invented only by someone visualising how a stone or some wood could be turned into a wheel. When the Spaniards invaded South America, they found a civilisation in many respects in advance of their own; the Aztecs had built cities, buildings and water irrigation systems using architectural techniques and mathematical expertise as advanced as any in Europe. Yet the Aztecs had not invented the wheel because no-one had visualised one.

It was only because Columbus could visualise the world as being round that he could set off to the west of Spain with the intention of finishing up to the east of it.

People were only able to develop the technology to land on the moon because they could first visualise someone stepping onto it. Cartoon strips, with such characters as Buck Rogers and Dan Dare, had seen the possibilities at a time when the technology did not exist.

So visualisation is the *first* practical step to achieving something—

▼————————————————————————

*Nothing at all can be achieved until someone first 'sees' or visualises the result*

————————————————————————▼

## How visualisation affects your mind—and your body!

Visualisation is like a camera. If the camera is out of focus, you will get a hazy picture. The best you get from a hazy picture is a hazy result. To avoid this, I write out my thoughts to crystallise them. I even write verses to sharpen up the images in my mind.

Crystal clear visualisation—visualisation in sharp focus—can have interesting results. If you are frightened enough of something, you only have to visualise it for your heart to beat faster, your body to heat up, a knot to form in your stomach, and perhaps your hands to shake. Yet it is only in your mind!

*I do an interesting experiment in my roadshows. I get everyone to close their eyes and to hold out their hand. 'Now, can you see me putting a lemon into your outstretched hand... Will you feel round the lemon... notice how rough and soapy the skin feels... Now I want you to find the sharp end and feel the rough nub of it... Now, will you take a knife into your other hand and cut into the lemon... Can you imagine the juice spraying out and smell the sharp tang as the knife cuts in?... Now I want you to cut a quarter out... The juice is running over your fingers as you cut... Now will you put the quarter up to your mouth and suck the juice...' By now, there will not be many people in that audience who are not experiencing a rush of saliva—yet the lemon does not even exist!*

...Except, that is, in their visualisation.

If it is possible for me to make your body chemistry react with my words, how much more could you do with your *own* thoughts? Just imagine if your whole mental and physical being were focused on a crystal clear vision of your goal—how long would it be before you attracted success? Just as it is said that money attracts money, so success gravitates towards success.

### How to develop belief in your vision

We have an expression, 'Seeing is believing'. Belief is nothing to do with what is actually the case, belief is what you *think*, *see* or *visualise* is the case.

Visualisation is a tool to help you to succeed. If you want a particular type of car, not only must you visualise exactly what that car is *but you must also visualise the action and work plan to earn the money you need to get that car*. It is this second step that is omitted by many teachers of visualisation, but it is vital if you want to get good results.

The classic here is when people say, 'It can't be done'. And then some 'idiot' goes and does it anyway because no-one told him or her it was *supposed* to be impossible.

It is belief that directs action. If you believe that something cannot be done, you will not act to make it happen; but, if you have seen in your mind's eye that you can do it, you will.

Therefore, it is important to spend time on visualising the things you want to achieve. But you do not visualise them as being in the future:

▼─────────────────────────────

### *You visualise them as happening* **now!**

─────────────────────────────▼

As I said at the start of this book, successful people *see* their success right from the beginning. That is, they avoid wasting time on visualising the problems; instead, they visualise the solutions. More important, they see what they are aiming for in sharp focus, in great detail. Their success is as real to them as if it had already happened, so they have a real *belief* that it can be achieved. Such powerful visualisation is not easy but it is worth the effort.

As I have said, the important thing about visualisation is to see things as *now*. Your subconscious mind is very literal. If you see things as happening now, it will work to make them come true now. But if you see things as in the future that is where they will stay—in the future.

Most people have a problem with 'seeing' something as if it is already true but visualisation is neither true nor false; it is simply a tool. A hammer and a chisel are neither true nor false, they are tools for a purpose.

Try this little exercise and see how you get on:

*Sit upright, but as comfortably as you can. Put your finger-tips together in front of you, just above your* *lap. Now close your eyes. Visualise something you really want—it doesn't matter what it is, but it must be something you really, badly want. Once you can see its colour and shape, start to repeat to yourself in a whisper, 'It's **mine**!'—each time seeing the words coming out of the vision. Keep saying this, with greater conviction and authority each time, all the time concentrating on the vision in front of you. Say this about ten times, then open your eyes.*

How do you feel? People describe the feeling they have in many ways but, if you have done it right, always with a good feeling! This is a great exercise to repeat when, as happens with all of us, doubts creep in.

### Set a time-frame for your vision

Apart from visualising your goal, you should also visualise yourself taking each step along the way. This will allow you to 'see' your actions in sequence and also the potential stumbling-blocks as they arise. It is dreaming with logic.

If you want to achieve promotion at work, visualise when you want to achieve it by. What steps will you need to take to achieve it by then? Set your calendar dates and these should be part of a new visualisation exercise in how to achieve your goal. By doing this, you avoid your aim always being sometime in the future. Instead, you have primed your subconscious to achieve it by a certain date.

The calendar dates you set to achieve your goals are important. Let's say you fix on a calendar date to achieve a promotion, for example, three years from now, but you actually have the potential to achieve it in six months. By setting the date too far ahead, you may well hold yourself back.

Conversely, if you set it for six months but the real potential is more likely three years ahead, this may actually be counter-productive to your success. Setting an impossible target may make you less successful than you would otherwise have been. An impossible target may mean that part of you does not believe you have the potential to achieve it in that time and that part of you will therefore reject your visualisations. Remember that, although you should use emotion to dream, you should plan logically.

If you do not achieve your goals by the date you have set, this does not mean that you have failed. If they were realistic within the parameters I have set above and if you had a genuine belief in your potential to achieve them in that time, the chances are that you will still achieve them more quickly than you might otherwise have done—and that actually means that you were successful because you got there more quickly than you would have done otherwise. Your goal was right, your effort was right—just the time-frame you allowed was incorrect. No big deal.

## The benefits of visualisation

So visualisation is a very important catalyst to achieving what you want. Many of you reading this are already high achievers or hard workers—if not workaholics! Hard though you already work, you will achieve what you want a lot quicker—you will even achieve more than you believe possible right now—if you spend less time on work but use that time on visualising or 'seeing' it through in sequence.

The clarity of your purpose will pull you towards your goals with less effort, with less determination, with less distraction and with less will-power. The great achievers do more with less effort than the rest of us. They work longer hours with less fatigue, not because they have more stamina than we do, but because they can visualise their plans, actions and goals better.

▼——————————————————————————

*Visualisation keeps you focused*
*Visualisation keeps you positive*
*Visualisation helps you to plan*

——————————————————————————▼

If you have to use will-power or determination to keep going, either what you are striving for is not what you *really*, deep-down want to do, or you do not have a crystal-clear, powerful image of what you want to achieve, or you cannot visualise your ability to achieve it.

▼——————————————————————————

*Proper visualisation always means that*
*you will go further faster than you would*
*have done otherwise*

——————————————————————————▼

But it should not replace planned hard work. Planned hard work will always achieve more than any spark of genius. So visualisation on its own is not a guarantee that you will reach your goal, only that you will get closer than you would have done without it.

# CHAPTER 16

# Now Plan Your Future!

Having read *my* book, I now want you to plan, on exactly the lines I show you in the following pages, where you want *your* life to go. Your planning book should be A4 size, using a good quality ring binder. And the title of your book?

MY PERSONAL PLANS

BY

(Your Name)

Your book will be in six sections and I'll show you how to fill in each section.

### How to complete Section One: 'What I Want'

(read in conjunction with page 126)

All of your aspirations in life, no matter what they are, will fall into one of three headings. They are all:

- Something you want to do, *or*

- Something you want to be, *or*

- Something you want to have.

Until you know what you want to do, who or what you want to be, or what you want to have, you cannot set out on a course of action. So the first thing we do in your Personal Planner is to write down everything you have ever wanted under these three headings.

This is an exercise in dreaming! It is very important that you do not consider the practicalities or possibilities of achieving your dreams, nor must you look at the logic of what you choose. If you do, you will be viewing yourself from where you are now, not from where you are going to be.

Most people, if asked to buy a car, will not always choose what they would really like to have, but what they think they can realistically afford now. The purpose of what we are going to achieve together is not what you can realistically afford—in any part of your life—or what you think you can realistically do, or what you think you can realistically achieve, but what you really, deep-down, want for *yourself*; only there lies true achievement, genuine success or absolute fulfilment. So give yourself permission to let all your barriers down and to be creative and imaginative. Dream away!

This exercise is important for another reason: it is a way of flushing out what you do *not* want. We spend a large amount of time, energy and focus in day-dreaming at the expense of what we *do* want to do! If something is not important enough to write down, it is not important enough for you to spend time on.

Remember that, if you want to keep your life round and balanced, you will need to choose aims in each of the six areas we looked at on page 107. You will attach different importance to different areas. That is fine; because our personalities differ, each area is not equally important to each of us. Nevertheless, to lead a balanced life, all of us need at least some serious aims in all areas.

Once you have written out your list, prune out anything which you do not feel a really powerful desire to achieve. If you would only 'quite like' something, that is not a strong desire, so cross it out! If you are not prepared to work hard to get it, cross it out because that is not a strong desire.

Beside all the aims you have left, write down the number '1'. If you number them 2, 3, 4 etc., you will psychologically attach lesser importance to them—so number every item '1'.

Next, put them in the order of priority in which they have to be achieved. For instance, you may have written down three aims:

• A car
• More money
• A new job.

But the order in which you may need to achieve them is:

• A new job
• More money
• A car.

Now note down which of the six life areas is affected and set the date for its expected achievement. As you achieve one goal, go for the next. Soon, so much excitement will be added to your life that, as one aim is reached, you will want to stretch out for the next! So it is important that you keep adding to your list, that you keep checking it and that you make it a regular part of managing your life's goals. But remember to start with *daily* goals (see page 106).

Your goals will change and it is normal and right that they do so. As you develop yourself, you will find that some things which you thought you wanted desperately will no longer matter to you, but other things will rise to take their place. No matter how much you dream, your current hopes are a reflection of your current knowledge and experience. As your knowledge and experience grow, so will the things you want for yourself.

This list has to be what *you* want and should not include goals which are more important to other people than they are to you. For this reason, do it in private because anyone else will influence you to leave things off or put things in to suit *them* rather than yourself. Once you have done it then by all means compile a joint list with a partner, spouse or child because, if their goals conflict with yours, this will give you the chance to talk it through before any problems arise. But, whoever you do goals with *must* have read this book. If they have not, they are not ready to set goals.

### How to complete Section Two: 'My Personal Priorities'

(read in conjunction with page 127)

From your list, 'What I Want', extract all the items which belong in the 'Physical & Health' area of your life. Then compare them carefully and decide which are the most important to you. Now write them down in the order in which you want to begin working on or for them.

Under each, write down the steps you intend to take to achieve them (see the examples on page 127).

You should now prepare the same 'My Personal Priorities' list for each of the other five areas of your life.

It is vital that your priorities reflect your own desires, values and standards, not those others think you should have. Because they are yours, priorities may be changed whenever this appears desirable to you. Priorities are valuable guides because they keep you on track to achievement.

More importantly, you will begin to 'see' the logic of achievement if your lists are set out in sequence.

### How to complete Section Three: 'What I Do Now'

(read in conjunction with page 128)

The next stage is to write down in as much detail as possible your own evaluation of your present level of achievement in the 'Physical & Health' area of your life. Include your strengths and accomplishments and any weaknesses you recognise. Knowing your present status will make it easier for you to see the proper road to take to reach your destination.

Be honest with yourself! If you are not, *you* are the only person you will fool. Until you know what your relative strengths and weaknesses are, you cannot know which of your traits you can rely on to attain your aims and which aspects of you could hold you back and will therefore need strengthening.

Once you have done this for one area of your life, you should prepare the same 'What I Do Now' list for each of the other five areas of your life.

### How to complete Section Four: 'Intermediate And Long-Term Goals For My Success'

(read in conjunction with pages 129)

Be sure to begin by working with *daily* goals. At a convenient time each day, review your Personal Priorities and choose a small and practical step you can take *that very day* to improve your life. Then put it in writing and *be sure to do it*! Next day, review how effective you were in achieving your target for the day before.

As you gain in confidence and begin to work with intermediate and long-term goals, you will need to put them into your 'My Personal Plans' book. Start with the goal which is highest in your order of priorities, in whichever of the six areas it is, and complete the 'Goals For My Success' chart. You have now chosen the single thing which matters most to you in this world.

As you complete each goal, make out a new 'Goals for My Success' for the next goal.

Depending on what goal you are going for, the time involved and the commitment needed to achieve it, you may be able to go for several goals at once. But, if a lesser goal means compromising the time and commitment you need to achieve a more important one, you have taken on a goal too many!

### How to complete Section Five: 'Affirmations'

(read in conjunction with page 130)

Affirmations are *hourly* reminders. Read them, aloud if possible, to remind yourself of the importance of achieving your goals. *They must be written as if they are **already** true*, on separate cards for each area of your life, and kept with you. By supporting your goals and serving as powerful tools to help you strengthen or change your thoughts, attitudes and habits, they change what happens in your life.

### How to complete Section Six: 'Goals I Have Achieved'

(read in conjunction with pages 131–132)

People, by the act of focusing on new goals, can often forget how much they have already achieved, so noting down your successes is an important part of having a good self-image. You deserve recognition for every goal you achieve! Congratulating yourself for what you have already done will help you to achieve more in the future. It is an important part of feeling good and of recognising how successful you are.

### Now put your Inner Force to Work!

Right after winning the 1993 US PGA championship, golfer Paul Azinger was diagnosed as having cancer. After months of treatment, during which he suffered massive discomfort, he is playing golf again. At the time of writing, he is competing again at the very highest level. As he said, *'You can have cancer in any part of the body but there is no such thing as cancer of the spirit'*.

You now have the privilege of a very special knowledge. Ever since the dawn of time, when humankind first acquired the ability to shape life through conscious thought, countless millions of people have found success in their private and family lives, their business lives, their spiritual or their social lives by applying the power of the Inner Force through the application of attitude and habit. Most did it by accident but, whether by accident or design, all success— *all* success—in any part of your life can come only from the proper application of attitude and habit. This is the power in each and every one of us which you now know how to harness.

*Could this knowledge indeed not be called priceless?*

The fulfilment to be gained from leading a life *you* choose transcends everything else. This is the achievement which will allow you to say with pride: '*I* did that!' To you now falls the endeavour of putting this priceless knowledge into action. Doubts, worries and outside influences will attack you along the way but, as you achieve, so will these lessen. Nothing, not even negatives, are for ever and your answer to all things is action with courage.

Ordinary people become extraordinary by their deeds. Beethoven was deaf, Milton was blind, Sarah Bernhardt with an artificial leg, stump raw and bleeding, still trod the stage. My life would not be long enough to write the stories of all those ordinary people who achieved miracles with their lives. Let Wendy Walker (see page 45) stand for them all.

One and all harnessed their Inner Force and now so can *you!* The world, our country, our society, your family, all need winners and *you*, yes *you*, were born with that winning ingredient within you. Play your part, accept your challenge, carve your destiny, hold your head high—do it *NOW!*—and make my reward your achievement.

▼ ▼ ▼ ▼ ▼

## As To The Question Of Your Life—You Are The Answer

## As To The Extent Of Your Problems—You Are The Solution

## As To Your Fears, You Are Your Strength

## The Answer To The Question, 'How High Will I Go?' Is—At What Point Will You Stop?

▲ ▲ ▲ ▲ ▲

## Section One Of My Personal Plans

| What I Want | | | |
|---|---|---|---|
| Ranking | I Want... | Area of life | Date entered |
| | | | |
| | | | |
| | | | |
| | | | |
| | | | |
| | | | |
| | | | |
| | | | |
| | | | |
| | | | |
| | | | |
| | | | |
| | | | |
| | | | |
| | | | |
| | | | |
| | | | |
| | | | |
| | | | |
| | | | |
| | | | |
| | | | |

*Section Two Of My Personal Plans*

| |
|---|
| **My Personal Priorities In My Physical & Health Area** |
| **1.** ~~Want to lose a stone~~ |
| Cut out dairy and sugar |
| Exercise (see below) |
| |
| **2.** ~~Want to get fitter~~ |
| Join gym and do 2 workouts a week |
| Walk 3 miles a day |
| |
| **3.** |
| |
| |
| |
| **4.** |
| |
| |
| |
| **5.** |
| |
| |
| |

*Section Three Of My Personal Plans*

## What I Do Now In My Physical & Health Area

*Section Four Of My Personal Plans*

## Intermediate And Long-Term Goals For My Success

Goal:

I will reach my goal before:

These things stand between me and my goal:

I will overcome the obstacles by taking these actions:

Reaching this goal will benefit me in these ways:

Am I willing to invest this time and effort to obtain the expected benefits?  Yes ☐  No ☐

How am I doing?

| Date | Poor ☐ | Fair ☐ | Good ☐ | Great ☐ |
|------|--------|--------|--------|---------|
| Date | Poor ☐ | Fair ☐ | Good ☐ | Great ☐ |
| Date | Poor ☐ | Fair ☐ | Good ☐ | Great ☐ |

*Section Five Of My Personal Plans*

# Affirmations:
# Physical & Health Area

**Sample Affirmation**

I feel and act
energetic and healthy

**Sample Affirmation**

I enjoy daily exercise

I feel *great!*

**Sample Affirmation**

Every day, I eat
correct and proper
food to stay healthy

**Sample Affirmation**

I wake up alert,
enthusiastic and
excited about each
new day

**Sample Affirmation**

My physical health is
always in tune with
what is required to
achieve my goals

*Section Six Of My Personal Plans*

## Goals I Have Achieved

| | Date achieved |
|---|---|
| **Financial & Career Area:** | |
| | |
| | |
| | |
| | |
| | |
| | |
| **Physical & Health Area:** | |
| | |
| | |
| | |
| | |
| | |
| | |
| **Mental & Educational Area:** | |
| | |
| | |
| | |
| | |
| | |
| | |

*Section Six Of My Personal Plans (continued)*

## Goals I Have Achieved

| | Date achieved |
|---|---|
| **Family & Home Area:** | |
| | |
| | |
| | |
| | |
| | |
| | |
| **Spiritual & Ethical Area:** | |
| | |
| | |
| | |
| | |
| | |
| | |
| **Social & Cultural Area:** | |
| | |
| | |
| | |
| | |
| | |
| | |

## An Invitation From The Author

Derek Ross is keen to hear from you about how you get on with the ideas in this book. If you would like to share your experiences, please write to:

*Derek Ross*
*Insight Publishing*
*3a The Maltings*
*Ross-on-Wye*
*Herefordshire*
*HR9 7YB*

## Business Seminars by Derek Ross

If everyone in your organisation actually *did* what you have already trained them to do, *could you handle the extra business that would result*? The best training and systems are of little benefit unless your people are *motivated* to use them. Derek Ross offers a range of highly effective seminars designed to unleash the motivational power of the Inner Force within your business. For information, please write to the publishers at the address above or ring:

*01989-564496*

## Orders & Volume Discounts

To order further copies, and for information on generous discounts for volume orders, ring the Insight orderline on:

*01989-566600*